*Daughter Zion Talks Back*
*to the Prophets*

## Society of Biblical Literature

## Semeia Studies

**General Editor:**
Gale A. Yee

Number 58

DAUGHTER ZION TALKS BACK
TO THE PROPHETS
A Dialogic Theology of the
Book of Lamentations

Carleen R. Mandolfo

# Daughter Zion Talks Back to the Prophets

## A Dialogic Theology of the Book of Lamentations

Carleen R. Mandolfo

Society of Biblical Literature
Atlanta

DAUGHTER ZION TALKS BACK
TO THE PROPHETS
A Dialogic Theology of the
Book of Lamentations

Copyright © 2007 by the Society of Biblical Literature

**Library of Congress Cataloging-in-Publication Data**

Mandolfo, Carleen.
    Daughter Zion talks back to the prophets : a dialogic theology of the book of Lamentations / By Carleen R. Mandolfo.
        p.   cm. — (Society of Biblical Literature Semeia studies ; v. 58)
Includes bibliographical references and index.
ISBN 978-1-58983-247-3 (alk. paper)
    1. Bible.    O.T.    Lamentations—Feminist    criticism.    2. Bible.    O.T. Lamentations—Criticism, interpretation, etc. 3. Bible—Postcolonial criticism. 4. Feminism—Religious aspects—Judaism. 5. God (Judaism) 6. Metaphor in the Bible. I. Title.

BS1535.52.M36 2007b
224´.306—dc22                                                                                    2007018763

14 13 12 11 10 09 08 07     5 4 3 2 1

Printed in the United States of America on acid-free, recycled paper conforming to ANSI/NISO Z39.48-1992 (R1997) and ISO 9706:1994 standards for paper permanence.

*To Professor Barbara Green,*
*Professor Robert Coote,*
*and Professor John H. Hayes—*
*mentors who saw more in me*
*than the evidence suggested!*

# Contents

# Acknowledgments

My revised dissertation (*God in the Dock: Dialogic Tension in the Psalms of Lament*) raised unintended questions about biblical authority. What started as an exegetical phenomenological inquiry into voicing and cultic contextual questions in psalms of lament quickly led into questions of theological interest. Honestly, I had always had very little interest in biblical theology because even the best of it (and there are many exceptional biblical theologies, of course) seemed too systematized and univocal for my taste. In trying to make sense of the data I was acquiring regarding voicing changes in the lament psalms, I read Walter Brueggemann's *Theology of the Old Testament*, and two things happened: it gave me a theological language for the linguistic data I was sorting through; and it made me realize that biblical theology does not have to try to wrestle the disparate biblical voices into a "coherent" system. Professor Brueggemann assured me that "God understood what I was doing" and encouraged me to continue my dialogic hermeneutics.

Along more theoretical and less explicitly theological lines, I'm especially grateful to Barbara Green, both for the assessment of Mikhail Bakhtin's work that she has provided to biblical scholars, and more personally for sharing her insights with me as they pertain to this book. Also due thanks are the members of the Lenox Colloquium who read and offered elaborate and thoughtful comments on chapter 1: Jacq Lapsley, Carolyn Sharp, Chip Dobbs-Allsopp, J. J. M. Roberts, Kathryn Roberts, and Scott Starbuck. I am sure I did not heed the suggestions made by these folks to the degree I should have, but the book is still better than it would have been without them. Colby College's generous sabbatical funding during 2004–05 provided the time to write the bulk of this book.

Finally, I am indebted to my research assistants who turned my haphazard research and writing habits into something intelligible, especially Dori Ellowitch, who has not surprisingly gone on to a career in publishing—her authors are lucky to have her—and Chris Holcombe for his careful and keen proofreading.

# 1

# Introduction

*Lamentations hardly needs interpretation for peoples who live in the ruins of destroyed cities, whose societies are decimated by genocide, or who barely subsist in the face of famine and poverty.* (Kathleen O'Connor, *Lamentations and the Tears of the World*)

## A Dialogic Hermeneutics

In the second chapter of Hosea, God makes this poignant promise to his people:

> In *that day*, I will respond (ענה)        —declares YHWH—
> I will respond to the sky,
> And it shall respond to the earth;
> The earth shall respond
> With new grain and wine and oil,
> And they shall respond to Jezreel.
> . . .
> And I will say to Lo-ammi, "You are My people,"
> And he will respond, "You are my God." (Hos 2:23–25)

All creation co-responding is evocative of the dialogic philosophies of both Mikhail Bakhtin and (the more overtly religious) Martin Buber. Are we to construe "that day" as having been accomplished in the biblical text, or is it merely an eschatological mirage? Using this text from Hosea as a sort of touchstone, this study will explore the question of divine-human (and ultimately human-human) relationality by bracketing off one particularly challenging phase in the relationship—played out between certain prophetic texts (Hosea, Jeremiah, Ezekiel, and Second Isaiah) that utilize the marriage metaphor to tell the tale of God and Israel from the "husband's" perspective, and the first two chapters of Lamentations in which the "wife" talks back.[1] Buber's dialogic philosophy, and more specifically the form it takes in Bakhtin's dialogic linguistics, informs every move I make in this study, although the connections will for the most part remain implicit. For Buber "dialogue" meant "existential encounter, meaningful exchange of selves, reciprocal revelation" (Kepnes: 31; 69).[2] Fundamental to both Buber and Bakhtin was an experiential ethic grounded in the face-to-face, or "I-thou," encounter. For them, in a "thou" relationship, the "other" should be allowed to work on us, get inside us, alter us (Kepnes: 25). In other words, an I-thou relationship moves beyond mere explanation—which for Buber was the hallmark of the "I-it" encounter—to empathy and under-standing. According to Buber, unfortunately, genuine I-thou moments are fleeting, eventually disintegrating into I-it encounters, or at least alternat-ing between these poles. It is important to note that their understanding of "other" included texts, and for Buber that meant especially the biblical text, which he understood as a *voice* more than a book (Buber 1964:869). Buber seemed to attribute to the biblical discourse a more pure I-thou account of divine interaction with humanity than I think can be supported (Buber 1967:67).[3] There are moments, to be sure—the dialogue between God and Abraham in Gen 18 over the fate of Sodom is, to my mind, one of the model dialogic theological moments in biblical discourse—but there are (many more?) moments when God and the people seem to be missing one another entirely, talking past, over, and around the other. The prophetic texts that feature the marriage metaphor are particularly tragic examples of Buber's I-it encounter.

The prophetic marriage metaphor figures the people Israel as a woman, God's wife, and even more specifically, an adulterous wife. The tracking of this metaphor through several prophetic texts and the Book of Lamentations results in an alternative history of the relationship between God and Israel, but because that history is rendered explicitly in intimate relational terms, specifically highly emotive speech, it cries out for a dia-logic hermeneutic. Of course, the patriarchal social arrangement in Israel precluded a genuine I-thou relationship within the institution of marriage (not that individual marriage units could not move past these structural restrictions), and this study will examine how the texts dependent on the gendered rhetoric of the divine-human relationship acquiesced to, negoti-ated with, and rebelled against these pressures.

---

1. Others have noted that Lam 1–2 is drawing on the prophetic marriage metaphor rhetoric (O'Connor 2002:20)

2. Buber's dialogic theology is presented in several places. See especially *I and Thou*. I appreciate Kepnes's reading of Buber because he puts Buber and Bakhtin into dialogue in ways that are useful to my goals.

3. But Buber was absolutely correct in his emphasis on the possibility of a never-ending I-Thou encounter between biblical text and reader (see *Werke II*, 847–71).

I nuance my primarily literary approaches with insights from some more explicitly political methodologies, namely feminist and postcolonial approaches. But these should not be thought of as models I *apply to* texts but rather useful conversation partners that can clarify certain points. Feminist and postcolonial criticisms provide a critique of Buber's and Bakhtin's emphasis on the reciprocity they understood as inherent in dialogic relationality, and which Buber specifically understood as constituting biblical discourse. Buber and Bakhtin failed, at least in explicit terms, to take into account the power dynamics that are at work in any dialogic encounter.[4] A feminist reading of the prophetic marriage metaphor and Lamentations 1–2 requires little justification—the gendered construction of Israel all but demands such an approach, and recently feminist scholars have been hard at work on these texts (especially the prophetic texts). As many studies have implicitly noted, the prophetic discourse in which the marriage metaphor is embedded in no way constitutes any part of a genuine dialogue. Daughter Zion's identity is fully constructed from on high, by her "husband." Zion is denied any subjectivity and moral agency because in the prophetic texts God is unwilling to enter into genuine dialogue with her.[5] In this study I argue that it is hermeneutically and theologically illuminating (and ethically satisfying) to read Lam 1 and 2 as Zion's response to the closed and finalized portrait painted of her in the prophets, as her attempt to reclaim agency.

Less obviously, contextually, these texts are at the nexus of converging significations of power, many of which are constituted by imperial pressures (which obviously press issues integrally connected to subjectivity and alterity, concerns shared by Buber and Bakhtin).[6] Well prior to 587 B.C.E., Judah found itself caught between the superpowers of the ancient Near East—Assyria, Egypt, and Babylon (not to mention closer neighbors who were minor players, but who further complicated political dynamics). Although many of the particulars of the pressures these powers exerted on the Judahites are unrecoverable, we are well advised to read texts such as

---

4. Of course Buber recognized that there was a need for I-thou relationships to replace I-it relationships, and for this reason his philosophy has much to contribute to postcolonial discourse. He knew that our identity is caught up either way in the "other" (a subject I address in depth below), but one way leads to violence, the other to God, peace, salvation, community.

5. What Dale Patrick says of communal laments certainly holds for the Prophets and Lamentations, that there exists "an irreconcilable gap between the people, to the degree that the communal laments articulate their stance, and YHWH, as represented by the prophets" (176).

6. Even without an imperial context, Leela Gandhi, *Postcolonial Theory* (New York: Columbia University Press, 1998) 85, notes that some theorists use the term "'colonialism' very loosely to imply any relation of structural domination which relies upon a self-serving suppression of 'the heterogeneity of the subject(s) in question,'" a definition that could apply to these texts regardless of their context.

Lamentations, which explicitly arose from such pressures, with colonial models in mind. Kwok Pui-Lan reminds us that the Bible is much more than a religious document. It is also a "political text written, collected, and redacted by male colonial elites in their attempts to rewrite and reconcile with history and to reconceptualize both individual and collective identities under the shadow of the empires" (8–9). To say that Lam 1–2 was written by colonial elites may be debatable, but that the Bible as a whole presses an agenda in response to colonial pressures seems safe. Jon Berquist has argued that the Bible as a whole is a colonial text, having been authorized and supported by a Persian imperialist agenda. But as Kwok has argued, although "it was produced by the social group of colonial administrators and canonizers, wedged between empire and colony," it was infused with "postcolonial potential" (Kwok: 8). Berquist suggests that it is the duty of interpreters to decolonize the text by ferreting out those voices that "can be used against the imperializing ideologies of the canon" (26–27).

The texts that are the focus of this study—Jeremiah, Ezekiel, Second Isaiah, and Lamentations—are amenable to colonial and postcolonial readings: the deployment of the marriage metaphor in the Prophets can be understood as serving imperialist interests, while the way that same metaphor is reconceived in Lamentations seethes with "postcolonial potential." Postcolonial concerns can be read into the Prophets on two levels. The emphasis in prophetic/divine discourse on blaming and controlling a potentially f(r)actious population could function to serve imperial needs for a subdued colony. Furthermore, the relationship between God and Zion at times poses a striking resemblance to the troubled and complicated relations that exist between colonizer and colonized. A primary function of imperial discourse, in all its forms, is to be the sole arbiter of meaningful subjectivity. Like imperial discourses, divine discourse in many prophetic texts serves to "tell individuals what exists, what is possible, what is right, what is wrong" (Berquist: 25).

Postcolonial and feminist interests converge in these texts as they use "the deployment of gender in the narration of identity, the negotiation of power differentials between the colonizers and the colonized, and the reinforcement of patriarchal control" (Kwok: 9) in their theological constructions. Specifically, I unpack the representation of gendered and colonial power relations by attending to the speech, including structure and content, of God and Zion in the texts that depend on the marriage metaphor.[7] Because the focus is on this metaphorical relationship, and not explicitly on Israel's relationship with foreign powers, God becomes the

---

7. Nancy Lee has recently focused on voicing in Jeremiah and Lamentations in order to determine whether the voices of the prophet and the city/Jerusalem in Jeremiah are rhetorically the same as the voice of the "narrator"/"prophet" and the city/Daughter Zion in Lamentations.

primary focus of postcolonial and feminist interrogations of these particular texts. It is often difficult in Lam 1–2 to distinguish between God and the (foreign) "enemies" in Daughter Zion's vitriol.

With the methodological particulars explicitly named, I can come clean about my ultimate goals. My hope is to contribute to the dethroning of biblical authority as it is now construed. Obviously, much work has already been done in this direction by liberation readers and "deconstructionists" of all stripes, but rather than diminishing biblical authority, per se, I want its centrifugal tendencies—its "unfinalizability" to use a clumsy Bakhtinian term—to be the source of its authority.[8] I want it to resound as the "words" of God, rather than the "Word."[9] With keen insight into the postmodern dilemma facing biblical scholars, M. Coleridge writes of the importance of transforming the myth of biblical authority: "Scripture may be the word of God, but the biblical God has many voices and they all speak at once: God speaks polyphonically" (19). If we care about justice, we must be careful not to approach the Bible, in Bakhtinian terms, as the monologic "word of the father" that in the end justifies divine violence (as many commentators are quick to do) (O'Connor 2002:116).[10]

---

8. Central to Lyotard's idea of postmodernism is the notion that emancipatory discourses are no longer possible because there is no longer a belief in the truth of foundational meta-discourses (e.g., about truth, justice, progress, etc.), but I believe that emancipation is in part achieved through the recognition that no one has an exclusive license on the truth; I agree, though, that a dialectic understanding of progress or liberation is wrongheaded.

9. For comparative purposes, I do not align myself with those who attribute to the Bible no moral authority, even when they recognize its cultural influence. Mieke Bal, for example, claims to be interested only in the "cultural function of one of the most influential mythical and literary documents" (Bal: 1). I take the moral authority of the Bible as a fact, whether for good or ill.

10. See, for example, the fairly recent "popular" commentaries by R. Davidson and R. K. Harrison. This is obviously more of an issue for those biblical theologians for whom the Bible constitutes an authoritative text in matters of faith. But even among such scholars, there is more and more attentiveness to the complexities of biblical authority. For an example of three prominent scholars who understand how important it is to resist monologizing hermeneutical tendencies, see W. Brueggemann, W. Placher, and B. Blount, *Struggling with Scripture* (Louisville: Westminster John Knox Press, 2002). Even among these thoughtful scholars, however, one senses a real resistance to any kind of ultimate hermeneutical dialogism. In his essay in this collection, Brueggemann, for example, explains, "[W]hile I believe in the indeterminacy of the text to some large extent, finally the Bible is forceful and consistent in its main theological claim. That claim concerns the conviction that the god who creates the world in love redeems the world in suffering and will consummate the world in joyous well-being" (11). The notion that a "main theological claim" inheres in the Bible seems highly problematic and renders all calls to dialogic interpretation disingenuous. One could argue for other equally "main" theological assertions in the Bible, such as the god who

> The authoritative word is located in a distanced zone, organically con-
> nected with a past that is felt to be hierarchically higher. It is, so to speak,
> the word of the fathers. Its authority was already acknowledged in the
> past. It is a prior discourse. It is therefore not a question of choosing it from
> among other possible discourses that are its equal. It is given (it sounds) in
> lofty spheres, not those of familiar contact. Its language is a special (as it
> were, hieratic) language. It can be profaned. It is akin to taboo, i.e., a name
> that must not be taken in vain. (Bakhtin 1981:342)

Biblical authority, rather, should inhere in the recognition that biblical discourse is a projection of a never-ending cosmic dialogue (which Bakhtin
called "Great Time"), "in which no meaning dies" and new meanings are
ever born (Claassens: 131).

An effective way to accomplish the loosing of the word from the "father" is to interrogate/deconstruct the father's discourse, specifically. This
means granting signifying power to several voices, ensuring that none has
intrinsic authority over the others.[11] T. Fretheim, for example, stresses a
relational approach to theology with an emphasis on the often challenging, but ultimately redeemed relationship between God and creation.
However, in the end he is not interested in allowing a single voice that
challenges divine hegemony to have any genuine persuasive power. For
him, humans bring disaster on themselves through their disobedience. In
the chapter on prophetic rhetoric he proclaims that God is merely the "me-
diator" of the consequences of sin. Furthermore,

> God's salvific will remains intact in everything, and God's gracious con-
> cern is always for the best; but in a given situation the best that God may
> be able to offer is burning the chaff to fertilize the field for a new crop.
> (165)

This may be comforting information for some or even many people. But
try telling this to the victims of the Nazi genocide. A dialogic approach

---

creates the world, constitutes it in division and otherness, which leads to endless
cycles of violence. If both of these are true, then neither is "main." But it must be
noted that Brueggemann (who is one of my primary inspirations for the dialogic
hermeneutics I practice) has cautioned against simplistic affirmations of God's
goodness, and apropos of this study makes the claim that "Israel's relentless
tradition of complaint finds a way of destabilizing every grand positive claim"
(2000:102). And in the wake of 9/11, many biblical scholars, theologians, and other
church-related scholars are beginning to appreciate and mine the resources of the
biblical lament tradition as it teaches that challenges to divine authority can still
constitute genuine prayer (see S. Brown and P. Miller).

11. B. Green, a scholar well-versed in Bakhtinian hermeneutic practices, supports, as do I, I. Pardes's (4) aim of making more biblical voices audible, rather
than valorizing a hypothetical matriarchal past, as many feminists have tried to
do. It is important to retrieve the skeptical and anti-covenant voices as part of a
feminist reading agenda (Green: 152).

that takes into account such disconfirming experiences requires that all texts be open to intense interrogation, and that even the character of God, as well as the way he has been interpreted by traditional biblical theologians, is susceptible to critique.[12] So I treat YHWH as Y. Sherwood does (and as she understands Derrida as doing), and "as most literary critics do, not as an entity but as a construct of the text. [Derrida's] detachment from the systematic, univocal tradition of exegesis, in which Yhwh's actions are typically rationalized and defended, enables him to present an alternative picture of a character who is himself resistant to univocality and union" (Sherwood 1996:200).[13] To be clear then, mine is not a systematic account of the divine—it is a reading of a character that I think has potentially profound ethical implications for human relationality beyond the text. To speak of the god of the Bible is to make no claims about "God"; but at the same time such a focus does not preclude the fact that on the cultural level (both then and now) the two gods often overlap, nor does it preclude the possibility that the biblical characterization *points toward* some ontological truths. Part of the goal of this study is to remind readers that it can be dangerous to forget this distinction.

Although Bakhtin was essentially mute on the subject of gendered language, the implication of his dialogic hermeneutics for the patriarchal context of biblical discourse in general, and the marriage metaphor in particular, is that the words put in the service of maintaining patriarchal privilege are open to recontextualization.

> According to Bakhtin, the word is the most neutral sign in that it does not have a specificity in any sphere of ideological creation; it is a social sign open to the fulfillment of all kinds of ideological functions. . . . The fact that the word has been mainly or mostly put to use by a patriarchal discursive agency does not mean that discourse must remain forever patriarchal, as a deterministic view would imply. If, by contrast, the word women speak is the "oppressor's language," in the terms proposed by the Bakhtinian School it is a word which is not closed, not finite, a word which is subject to answerability. (Diaz-Diocaretz: 130)

Juxtaposing texts without the imposition of *a priori* prerogatives helps level the playing field.

> All utterances are alloys, many times over. None is monologically correct or in control; the plurality decenters the patriarchal control from any one person or group, avoids the sovereign and authoritative, the dichotomous

---

12. The Jewish midrashic tradition has a long history of challenging God, a result of its commitment to dialogic engagement with the divine as well as the tradition.

13. While this is indeed methodologically true of my approach, I do believe that the Bible is at some level revelatory of God as being, but for me, insofar as the Bible reveals anything about God, it reveals a vastly multidimensional God that is entirely resistant to iconography of all sorts—discursive or imagistic.

> and binary. . . . Bakhtin's insistence—flawed though it may have been in
> practice—that all construction is situational deprives the dominant angle
> from its claim to being natural and inevitable. (Green: 58)

The resulting non-systematic approach to biblical theology to which
Bakhtin's dialogic thinking contributes is preferred to the more systematic
dialectic approach that dominated the first one hundred years (and is not
finished yet) of biblical scholarship for reasons that J. Kristeva articulates.
Dialectic thinking is

> based on a triad and thus on struggle and projection, a movement of
> transcendence, and still firmly within Aristotelian logic. Dialogism, on
> the other hand, replaces these concepts by absorbing them within the
> concept of relation. It does not strive towards transcendence but rather
> toward harmony. . . . (Kristeva: 88)

If ensuring all a fair hearing has any priority in our ethics, then a contemporary biblical theology should prefer the paradigm shift toward
dialogism and relationality, over "truth," transcendence, or synthesis. "Of
course, even the dialogic is susceptible to unequal power relationships,
but, at least in principle, it respects alterity rather than seeking to synthe-
size or vanquish it" (Edelstein: 36).

My reading then is admittedly theologically (as well as textually)
deconstructive.[14] Deconstruction as an interpretive strategy has been over-
used, misused, and vilified, but I follow Y. Sherwood's (who I think does
deconstruction better than most biblical scholars) understanding of it as
an "attempt to draw out the text in its own logic and idioms, but also to
think about the limits of the text by holding it up to the scrutiny of its own
logic" (2004). Close scrutiny of divine discourse, more than most biblical
utterances, tests the limits of biblical logic in that the deity's words have
tended to set the hermeneutic agenda of most interpreters. "The task of
the deconstructionist . . . is to locate the hierarchies that the text is consciously promoting or unconsciously taking for granted and, by working
within them, to make the text 'insecure in its most assured evidences'"
(Sherwood 1996:174). This is in stark contrast to the aspirations of the traditional humanities.

> These various humanisms are . . . unified in their belief that underlying
> the diversity of human experience it is possible, first, to discern a uni-
> versal and given human nature, and secondly to find it revealed in the
> common language of rationality. (Gandhi: 27)

---

14. I am challenged by Kwok Pui-Lan's observation that those of us who
engage in deconstructive reading strategies too often seem unable to construct
new discourses about God (135). While I readily admit that my reading of God is
deconstructive at one level (i.e., works against the explicit intentions of the text),
at another level I am trying to suggest another reading strategy, a dialogic one,
which I hope people might find new and constructive.

In contrast, postmodernists insist that universalist notions of any kind are totalitarian and a potential threat to otherness and difference.

Ironically, we find this tension even in the emancipatory discourses, such as feminism and postcolonialism. I want to maintain a belief in the possibility of dialogue and progress, while at the same time recognizing that the journey there will be anything but linear and that in the end I might have to redefine my notion of "progress," which may no longer include consensus. The emphasis in this particular study, however, will be on dismantling the totalizing effects of certain biblical discourses rather than modeling a full-blown dialogue. In the case of traditionally authoritarian discourses, some deconstructive work has to be the first step toward genuine dialogue and progress; and perhaps dialogue is the only progress we can hope for.

Abandoning linear notions of progress should not, however, be considered nihilistic. I am not interested in "destructing" texts, of proclaiming them as ultimately meaningless; quite the opposite. I want to recognize that all texts, of necessity, must exclude elements, that all texts make choices, and that reading honestly and carefully requires attending to the exclusions, those things that the text omits or wants us to overlook.[15] Another way to put it is, Where does the biblical text fall short of its own ideals of justice? Attending to the exclusions, is, in my opinion, a crucial aspect of reading ethically. It is akin to Charles Cosgrove's hermeneutical principle of "counter-cultural awareness," a hermeneutic practice that puts emphasis on the "aniconic voices of scripture that speak for the less powerful." Rather than nihilistic, a focus on the texts' inherent, though implicit, subversiveness can be gratifyingly liberating. Deconstruction, Sherwood warns, should not, however, result in the replacing of one set of values with another; rather, it should irreparably rend the text (1996:174). While my reading of the marriage of God and Zion could be construed as one-sided in favor of Zion, taken as a whole with all previous readings, it should be seen as a small correction that does not come close to superseding the values previously placed on the text. Furthermore, the dialogic intentionality of my hermeneutic celebrates the interplay of discourses, without dialectic resolution. (Surely a god worthy of worship would applaud his own deconstruction to facilitate such goals!)

The notion of responsiveness between texts that make no explicit claim to be in dialogue needs some explication. To what degree can we establish an intention on the part of the poet of Lam 1 and 2 to respond to and rebuke particular claims made by the prophets? In this regard, a distinction needs to be made between explicit allusion and more reader-oriented

---

15. Kwok Pui-Lan states her goal as a postcolonial feminist reader is to "show what is silenced, suppressed, or glossed over" (108).

intertextual connections.[16] The former attempts to make diachronic, and sometimes even historical claims that maintain an interest in authorial intent, while the latter focuses on synchronic concerns that largely overlook intentionality to focus on text and reader.[17] When dealing with ancient texts it is particularly difficult to substantiate direct influence, unless it is explicitly acknowledged by the borrowing author. Furthermore, many connections have to do with shared genres and traditions, such as occurs when lament forms and vocabulary are found scattered throughout many biblical books. So, for example, in chapter 3 of this book, when I draw form-critical comparisons between lament psalms and Lam 1–2, I am not claiming that the poet of Lam 1–2 was intentionally borrowing from particular psalms, but I am interested to show how the poet reworked lament traditions, in general, for his purposes. In this case we can speak of "influence"—there may be some authorial intentionality, but it is not necessarily explicit and may not even be particularly conscious, and thus cannot be categorized as allusion, per se. Neither can it, however, be understood as a purely intertextual phenomenon insofar as there is a more significant connection between these texts than merely reader's prerogative or coincidental textual echoes. The connections I foreground between prophetic revelations and Lam 1–2 suggest some intentionality, more or less depending on the particular portion of text being examined.[18] I try to point to these possible intentionalities as we work our way through the comparisons. Still, while I do think there is telling evidence of actual allusion, polemic even (which Sommer describes as an instance of one text disputing or arguing with another), in the end my work would best be understood as a type of intertextuality. This is so for two reasons: the evidence I examine is rarely conclusive enough to make a definitive call regarding allusion, nor am I much interested in establishing dependence; and perhaps more important, I make connections between particular prophetic texts and Lamentations because in canonical and literary terms the texts themselves demand them, and because I think others' readings of these texts will be enriched by these associations.

This hermeneutic frame of mind is not unlike midrashic approaches to texts, which more and more are being recognized as having affinities with various postmodern hermeneutics. For the rabbis, words form a never-ending conversation, and putting textual voices into dialogue is the goal of

---

16. The following discussion of allusion and intertextuality depends to a significant degree on Sommer's work, especially chapter 1.

17. Tull Willey has an excellent discussion of the hermeneutical possibilities of intertextual reading (1997: ch. 2).

18. B. Sommer stresses how difficult it is to establish direct borrowing between Lamentations and Second Isaiah, for example, because of the typicality of lament forms and how frequently they occur in different cultural discourses. See chapter 4.

interpretation. Since midrashic approaches to texts model life in ways that traditional Christian hermeneutics beholden to rationalism do not, readers of the Bible should attend to them more. One Christian theologian and biblical scholar who employs midrashic techniques as a way to dialogue more genuinely with the Jewish tradition after the Shoah describes midrash in such a way that makes plain its relation to my approach: "[M]idrash is a style of interpretation that leverages the text in question by reference to similarly constituted texts in the canon. . . . In fact, in one text there are echoes . . . of other texts, traces of other stories that in the way they are incorporated offer subtle comparisons and contrasts and thereby invite commentary and critique" (Knight: 10). Overall, the principle impulse behind midrashic hermeneutics is to retrieve tradition for contemporary consumption, a goal that resonates with most nonhistorical biblical criticism, especially those approaches that are emancipatory in nature.

The Hosean text quoted at the beginning of this chapter is a step in the right direction toward meaningful dialogue, one of many biblical indicators that YHWH is attentive to the importance of reciprocal exchange. In the narrative portions of the Tanakh, especially, YHWH occasionally actively seeks dialogue with humans—Adam and Eve, Cain, Abraham in Gen 18, and so on. In the Psalms and Lamentations, the people seek him out, but a response is usually ambiguous or missing altogether. In Job, God famously responds to Job's lament, but the content of the response suggests that God has not exactly *heard* Job's plea. His revelations to the prophets are not exactly dialogue, but pronouncements in which he shuns dialogue, for the most part. In Ezek 20, YHWH goes out of his way to find an excuse not to respond to the people—he gives them bad laws that will defile them and then tells them that people who defile themselves do not deserve a response (vv. 25, 31). The suggestion that God set them up to fail is of course Ezekiel's rhetorical strategy for salvaging God's omnipotence. But to read the text theologically means we have to accept that we are not in a genuine relationship with God, are not independent subjects, but are rather manipulated to respond the way he thinks we will.[19] When the people in Ezek 20 voice an opinion and make a choice (to be like the other nations), they are not permitted—God will make their decisions for them by force. Similarly, Jeremiah is ordered not to intercede for "this people . . . I will not listen to you" (Jer 7:16). The result is that genuinely human voices in the prophets are rare and when they occur they are in the form of indirect discourse, which is subject to manipulation.

In the prophetic texts in which the marriage metaphor predominates, YHWH struggles—and ultimately fails—to listen. In a nod to the importance of dialogue, he (ostensibly) quotes the people several times and then re-

---

19. Obviously this is not the point Ezekiel is trying to make, nor even a valid question in his context; but it does lend credence to the point the people make in Ezek 18—that YHWH is unfair (vv. 25, 29).

sponds to his own quotes, of course all the time hearing in their words (vocalized through his mouth) only what he wants/expects to hear—all that he is capable of hearing, through his rage. The result is what you would expect when two human beings try to solve their problems one-sidedly—violence, whether physical, psychic, or emotional. God's view of the situation, as mediated through the prophets is, of course, very different. The prophets strain their vocal chords chastising the people for not listening. As most commentators are happy to affirm, the prophets are surely correct to a degree—undoubtedly the people fail to heed good advice and thus make poor decisions, some of which are partly to blame for the predicaments in which they find themselves. But a question reported by K. P. Darr of one of her students qualifies prophetic condemnation and in part drives this investigation: "Am I simply to accept the abusive husband's explanation of why his wife deserved to be murdered?" (109). We answer an undeliberative "yes" to this question at the Bible's (and to some degree our) peril. If taking the student's question seriously causes a reassessment of the Bible's privileged moral position, so be it. It seems to me, paradoxically, to be the only way to ensure the Bible's position as a serious moral interlocutor. The other option is to dismiss these troubling texts as irrelevant, an option I want to avoid for the reason Darr commends: "Sometimes, we continue to embrace hurtful texts not because we affirm their answers, but rather because they force us to confront the important questions" (117).

## Authoring: Narratives as Constitutive of Identity Formation

Now that I've sketched a broad outline of my hermeneutic philosophy, I want to discuss more specifically how a commitment to dialogism affects my approach to the texts featured in this study. As noted, the structure of Bakhtin's dialogic hermeneutic has an ethical dimension. The same dialogic relationship he outlined between author (and for him a reader was also an "author") and text, and text and text, extends into the realm of interpersonal relations. We are all constituted in part by our interactions with others. "Authoring" is Bakhtin's term for the architectonic work we are all involved in vis-à-vis each other. We are all the co-authors of each others' lives.[20] As a human being, I am "finished" by others; I have no independent identity apart from the "gaze" of others. Part of the job of

---

20. A. MacIntyre's dialogic ethics also makes this claim: "We are never more (and sometimes less) than the co-authors of our own narratives. . . . We enter upon a stage which we did not design and we find ourselves part of an action that was not of our making" (213). So for MacIntyre, we are constrained from telling whatever story about ourselves we would like because of "the fact of our participation in a narrative that began long before we were born and which contains many other characters" (Nelson: 55).

authoring others involves listening to them as *responsibly* as we can, listening and responding *fairly*.

> Authoring is the key action of human existence. I author my self; I am co-responsible for the shaping of others with whom I interact; and as an artist, I author a work of art—for present purposes, a literary hero, who will author others, and so forth. . . . I incline toward an other, live into his or her experience. I enter as deeply as I am able the space of the other—their particularity—perceive it to some extent with their eye or ear—and then return to my own space, remembering and marking—integrating—what I have experienced.[21] (Green 1984:33–34)

Our ability to author others has to do with the "surplus of vision" to which we are privy relative to the other (Holquist: xxii). When we author someone we construct a "narrative" of their life based on the information we have about them, as well as our own particularity. The narrative we construct has a direct bearing not only on our understanding of them, but on their self-understanding. Authoritative cultural narratives, what Hilde Nelson calls "master narratives," also have a part to play in our self-identities as well as in our conceptions and authoring of others (Nelson: 6–7).[22] Thinkers from many different disciplines have recognized the influence that cultural narratives have on human identity.[23] M. Foucault, for example, explains how myths come to affect the way we think of ourselves and others—they are among the most powerful identity-constituting cultural discourses. The way in which myths describe particular groups of people comes to affect the identity of those people because over time myths come to seem "natural," as descriptive of the way things and certain people "really are."[24] And insofar as members of a society buy into the mythic

---

21. K. Clark and M. Holquist call this interaction "friendly alterity" (Green 1984: 70).

22. "Master narratives are often archetypal, consisting of stock plots and readily recognizable character types, and we use them not only to make sense of our experience . . . but also to justify what we do. . . . As the repositories of common norms, master narratives exercise a certain authority over our moral imaginations and play a role in informing our moral intuitions. Our culture's foundation myths—the Passion of Christ, for example, or Washington Crossing the Delaware—are master narratives."

23. "The importance of narrative to the construction of a moral life is becoming widely understood by psychologists, religious studies scholars, sociologists and philosophers. They have produced a body of literature commonly called 'narrative ethics.' [N]arrative ethics accords a central role to stories, not merely employing them as illustration, example or ways of testing our intuition regarding moral theories or principles, but regarding them as necessary means to some moral end" (Nelson: 36).

24. Y. Sherwood's understanding of Barthes's definition of myth is also instructive here: " 'myth' is the semiotic expression of an ideology," the symbols of

worldview, their agency is largely dictated by the particulars of the myth, or some other authoritative narrative.

> [N]arratives figure prominently in the moral life: they cultivate our moral emotions and refine our moral perception; they make intelligible what we do and who we are; they teach us our responsibilities; they motivate, guide, and justify our actions; through them, we redefine ourselves. (Nelson: 70)

Thus, myths and all major cultural narratives are inherently ideological; they are in other words persuasive discourses (Benveniste: 208–9). This means, of course, that some dominant narratives may be "used by those in power to mold society in a certain way. These modes of discourse seek to construct people's subjectivity; that is, they seek to get people to define themselves in a certain way" (Shields: 62).[25] If we do not author responsibly (and that includes listening well)—in other words are not answerable for the stories we both read and tell—then the kind of authoring we do can cause damage. A person's agency can be seriously compromised by the types of stories we construct about them.[26]

Nelson has written extensively on the influence or the authoring power that master narratives have over our identities. Her definition of personal identity is dialogic in nature (and coincides with Bakhtin's dialogic ethics). It is

> a meaning-system that narratively represents, from one's own perspective and from that of others, the things that contribute importantly to one's life over time. As such, it cannot be intelligible only to me. To suppose that it could is to treat an identity as a kind of private language whose rules and syntax need not be accessible or meaningful to anyone else. That supposition misses the fundamentally social nature of systems of meaning. (103)

Nelson's understanding of how narratives function to construct identities contributes significantly to the way I will read the formation of Daughter Zion's identity at the hands of the prophets/deity as well as the way she tries to reclaim it.

> Personal identities are constituted by the complex interaction of narra-

---

which are put to the use of establishing and upholding the hegemonic values of a given culture (1996:108).

25. Foucault has argued that dominant discourses wield power only with the acquiescence of those whom they are trying to control. This is surely true to some extent. Many oppressed people collude in their oppression because of the persuasive power of dominant cultural narratives. But postcolonial criticism has convincingly shown that some oppressed people do not accept the dominant discourse, but are literally too powerless to openly oppose it.

26. For a linguistic explanation of how words "do things," see J. L. Austin's *How to Do Things with Words.*

tives from a first-, second-, and third-person perspective that create an understanding of who someone is. Many of the stories that constitute the identity from each of these perspectives are master narratives and fragments of master narratives—stories, drawn from the cultural store, that circulate widely within a society and embody its shared understandings. . . . Because master narratives are generic, they identify groups of people; individuals derive some portion of their identities from their membership in the group. Many master narratives are benign and indeed socially indispensable, since they figure heavily in our ability to make sense of ourselves and one another. Others are morally compromised or flat-out evil, because they unfairly depict particular social groups as lacking in virtue or as existing merely to serve others' ends. (152)

That humans are (or should be) answerable to one another is an ethical given for most, but what would it mean to claim that God is likewise answerable for his authoring? Does God, in fact, author Daughter Zion *responsibly*, or is his narrative *morally compromised?* Is he required to be answerable? The way we answer these questions can tell us much about what we expect from the divine-human relationship (and from one another, by implication).

The Bible as a whole, as well as its constituent parts, fits the definition of a master narrative.[27] It lays out, in mythic proportions, a schema for human and human-divine interaction. It has for millennia determined the cultural contours of entire societies and molded the identities of those who inhabit those societies. It determines social boundaries, empowering those on the inside of those boundaries and proscribing the agency of those on the outside. The story of God and Zion as it plays out in the Prophets is a microcosm of this process. These prophetic texts constitute mini–master narratives in their own right.[28] They uphold the normative worldview— patriarchal, monotheistic, and so on—of the Bible that distinguishes men from women and believers from apostates. As such, these prophetic representations do what many master narratives (unfortunately) do—they justify violence against those groups they characterize as somehow morally deficient. Daughter Zion, wife of YHWH, is cast as an adulterous woman, a degenerate "whore" who deserves the wrath of her lord, a lord the master narratives are careful to describe to us as just and merciful. The success of the prophetic rhetoric can be gauged by the centuries of interpretation

---

27. "[M]ost master narratives aren't so much stories as ensembles of repeated themes that take on a life of their own. Fragments of history, biography, film fables, jokes, and similar narrative forms ring changes on the theme, as do proverbs, music, advertising slogans, and other cultural artifacts. . . . The master narrative of the African-American Matriarch contains politician's speeches, *Amos 'n' Andy's* Ruby Begonia character, "The Saint Louis Blues," and other such items" (Nelson: 158).

28. It should be noted that when I refer to the prophetic "narrative" I am not alluding to a formal (i.e., generic), but rather a conceptual, designation.

that did not (and still often does not) think twice about condoning God's decision to obliterate his wife/his people. If the Bible is a master narrative that continues to support the patriarchal master narrative of ancient Israel, then it is not difficult to see why we are so easily taken in. Its view of things seems natural and inevitable.

The prophetic marriage metaphor is one instantiation of Israel's master narrative that says women are "naturally" inferior to men and must defer to them in all matters social and moral. Because it taps into a vein that goes deep into Israel's understanding of itself, the marriage metaphor is part of an extremely effective rhetorical strategy deployed by the prophets. I say more about just how this metaphor functions in Hosea, Jeremiah, and Ezekiel in chapter 2. But it suffices for now to say that YHWH's and his prophets' construction of Zion is problematic first and foremost because it lacks reciprocity. *God does not author responsibly.* He "tells stories" about her that entirely disregard her point of view. It is also structurally problematic—her words are aired only through his mouth. And in terms of content, the words he chooses for her serve only his self-interests. This arrangement is naturalized because of the master narrative that undergirds it. Because master narratives make their way into every nook and cranny of a society and "lodge there tenaciously," they can begin to be denaturalized or made "strange" only under the pressure of our postmodern "hermeneutics of suspicion" (Nelson: 159).[29]

A hermeneutics of suspicion is itself a component of one of our master narratives—one that heralds the "death of the author" and proclaims that notions of transcendence and ultimate authority are suspect. That does not mean that we are now in a position to celebrate the demise of patriarchy. Seemingly conflicting master narratives can exist side by side in society (consider the "wrath of God" vs. the "mercy of God"). They blend and clash to varying degrees, but in the end together make up the fabric of our social and personal identities and beliefs. As expressed by Nelson, many master narratives are "socially indispensable" since without them we would be unable to make sense of our world and our place in it. However, as has also been noted, some master narratives can "damage" those it renders as morally lacking.

> The connection between identity and agency poses a serious problem when the members of a particular social group are compelled by the forces circulating in an abusive power system to bear the morally degrading identities required by that system. These mandatory identities set up

---

29. A recent and ongoing example of how master narratives can be dislodged by competing master narratives is the current situation of gay rights in Western societies. Gay rights are gaining ground as fast as they are only because there is another master narrative about freedom and equality in this country that is assisting it. On the other hand, of course, gay rights are still constrained by the master narrative of Christian "natural law."

expectations about how group members are to behave, what they can know, to whom they are answerable, and what others may demand of them. Here we may speak of *damaged* identities. (Nelson: xii)

By definition (or most definitions, at least), God, as creator (i.e., ultimate author), determines the extent of our right to autonomous existence. In the story of Israel and God, he sets the rules. Indeed, he quite literally wrote the "contract." God's power over his people is homologous to male privilege over women, so it is not surprising that, in terms of the metaphorical depiction of their relationship, God's authoring of Zion takes the form it does.

In the prophets, God dictates how Zion should behave, what she is allowed to know (through indirect discourse he determines her epistemic boundaries), to whom she owes allegiance, and so on. By all accounts then, hers is a "damaged" identity. But insofar as Zion is injured by stories, we have reason to believe that stories can, likewise, reconstitute her sense of self.

> [B]ecause identities are narratively constituted and narratively damaged, they can be narratively repaired. The morally pernicious stories that construct the identity according to the requirements of an abusive power system can be at least partially dislodged and replaced by identity-constituting stories that portray group members as fully developed moral agents.[30] (Nelson: xii)

Having said all this, Nelson makes the important point that we are not the only legitimate arbiters of our identities. This logically follows from the dialogic notion of identity I have been advancing thus far, but could use some elaboration.

> Just as we construct self-constituting stories around the aspects of ourselves and our lives we care most about, so *others* construct identity-constituting stories around the aspects of our lives *they* care most about. . . . And sometimes these others interpret a feature of our lives very differently from the way we interpret it, which is to say that they construct different stories, with different plots and from different points of view, around that feature. . . . [S]elf-knowledge is fallible, so there are gaps and distortions in my understanding of who I am. This is an *epistemic* consideration. But there are *practical* reasons why other people's stories about me are sometimes more authoritative than my own: who I am depends to some extent on who other people will let me be. And finally, there are *conceptual* grounds for denying that I hold trumps: my identity is always contingent in part on others, because personal identities are necessarily social or interpersonal. . . . I cannot be the sole arbiter of the stories that constitute

---

30. The notion of counterstory connects to some degree with Brueggemann's theology of "countertestimony," except that his is more dialogic and hers more dialectic. In other words, Brueggemann's idea does not necessarily embrace the necessity of resolving anything.

> me. . . . Our self assessment can be plagued by "ignorance" and "mistakes about our motives, intentions and beliefs"; we are prone to "self-deception" and we tell ourselves "flat-out lies." (82, 99)

Accordingly, I want to be careful to avoid the mistake of dismissing out of hand God's assessment of Zion simply because it is not her assessment. In light of their long history together, YHWH has a surplus of vision with regard to Daughter Zion that positions him advantageously for assessing her.[31] So, his words do not simply construct her *ex nihilo*, but they may be assumed to have some basis in experience. However, Nelson goes on to say that all things being even, there is reason to privilege self-assessment over third-party assessment.

> While it's true that the actions that express who I am require uptake on the part of others for their completion, it's also true that these others stand in a different relation to my acts from me. I initiate them; I intend and endorse them; I bring it about that my past actions come to mean something, or something different, in light of my further actions; I am responsible for much of what I do. Indeed, it's because I am the person most closely identified with my actions that they reveal who I am. For these reasons, if the backward-looking stories I weave around what I've done are acceptable according to the credibility criteria, then they should be acknowledged to have a certain authority over others' equally acceptable but different stories about who I am. (104)

An intertextual reading of Zion's speech in Lam 1–2 with Jeremiah and Ezekiel will demonstrate that her words reveal a personal continuity between her past actions and her assessment of her current situation, and may be found credible enough to deserve due consideration. For this reason, at the very least, we are obliged to privilege Zion's story. Furthermore, generations of scholarship have ignored or denied the legitimacy of her perspective, so fair play requires the rectification of this imbalance.

One of the first tasks of a counterstory is to challenge the master narrative by retelling the story in "such a way as to make visible the morally relevant details that the master narratives suppressed" (Nelson: 7). In Lam 1–2, the details that Zion privileges, which were previously passed over by YHWH, have mostly to do with the tremendous suffering she is experiencing. Her position makes clear, first and foremost, that no matter the gravity of her sin, it cannot have mandated such a severe punishment, and second, that her allegedly objectionable actions are not as morally black and white as YHWH suggests.

Bakhtin claimed that all discourse is involved in co-authoring activities—human-human, human-text, text-text, and so on—but it seems fair

---

31. "I can see some facets of the others that they cannot see of themselves; I have a *surplus of vision* (or of seeing) in regard to an other, as of course any other has as well in relation to me" (Green 2000:41; see also Bakhtin 1990:15–22).

to wonder about the legitimacy of mutual authoring in terms of the divine-human relationship. That God authors (indeed, creates) humans is a given. But how can one speak of humans authoring God? The Bible seems our best witness to and model of that process. As Brueggemann's theology testifies, all that can be known of YHWH resides in the words spoken to and about Him (1997:xv–xviii, 145). This is not to make an ontological claim, but to recognize that inasmuch as God spoke the cosmos into existence, so too do humans speak God into existence every time they read and reflect on previous words spoken about Him. As Green notes, "The interpenetration of divine persons and of the human and divine elements permits neither isolated sovereignty nor abased self-annihilation. Bakhtin denied both that one participant stands alone and also that the other is swamped" (30). The partial purpose of constructing a dialogic theology for these texts is to remind readers of this in regard to Daughter Zion. The focus on the construction of God's identity serves not only a theological, but an ethical purpose. It achieves an important goal in (post)feminist thinking having to do with Spivak's injunction that feminist scholars turn their attention to "man" as object (rather than woman, as feminism has traditionally done) and thereby reinfuse women with subjectivity. Spivak proposes that the feminist deconstructivist must ask: "what is man that the itinerary of his desire creates such a text?" (Spivak: 186).[32] In this way, woman can be restored to the position of the questioning subject. It appears Zion beat us to this punch by more than two thousand years.

## A Dialogic Theology

The reading approaches outlined above ultimately result in a dialogic theology that provides humanity an avenue for speaking honestly to God about their experience of him. It is a theology that makes demands upon God. In his study of lament psalms, Brueggemann finds biblical precedent for this impulse.

> [T]he lament psalms insist upon Israel's finding voice, a voice that tends to be abrasive and insistent. The lament psalm is a Jewish refusal of silence before God. . . . It is a Jewish understanding that an adequate *relationship with God permits and requires a human voice that will speak out against every wrong perpetrated either on earth or by heaven.* . . . I consider this matter of voice and violence not to be a theoretical issue but a concrete, practical, pastoral issue because we live in a violent, abusive society in which there is a terrible conspiracy in violence that can only be broken when the silence is broken by the *lesser party.* (2001:22, emphases mine)

---

32. Of course, she goes on to say that this "gesture must continue to supplement the collective and substantive work of 'restoring' woman's history and literature" (186).

It follows that readings of biblical texts that permit the voices of the "lesser parties" a moment in the limelight can have real-life repercussions for how we attend to our own lesser parties.

In terms of authoring, a dialogic theology suggests that we reflect to God an aspect of himself that he is not aware of or attending to. It is a theology that goes beyond description to suggest that God is mutable and in process, as are we—that we can author God as surely as he does us.[33] There are a number of examples of this in the narrative sections of the Bible, and the psalms imply it, but traditional biblical theology stays focused on static, rather than relational, descriptions of God.[34] Rarely is the Bible's God described as genuinely relational, that is, capable of mistakes and open to the ways in which we need him to rethink his piloting of this ship. Even those who are willing to posit relationality as one of God's primary attributes in the Bible are less willing to explore the darker side of the divine-human relationship. For example, in response to Brueggemann's suggestion that there might be a chink in God's fidelity to humanity, Fretheim says "God's fidelity in the relationship need not be brought into question just because the *human* party to the relationship can decide to be unfaithful, break the relationship, and suffer the consequences. Nor is that faithfulness compromised by divine judgment" (Fretheim: 21).

Even for a theologian who is as concerned to put the stress on a relational theology as Fretheim, there is a deep-seated resistance to holding God accountable for failures in the divine-human relationship.[35] Real relationship, however, should be predicated on reciprocity, not on a covenant of power and hierarchy.[36] A dialogic theology demands genuine reciproc-

---

33. This notion is reminiscent of one of the tenets of Jewish mysticism known as *tikkun olam*, which posits that humans are partners in God's creative intentions that have yet to reach fulfillment. Plaskow points out how empowering this notion can be for women in a story about a women's theological conference in 1972 in which God was ultimately defined as "Being," rather than "a Being" (143–44).

34. Theologians of a more philosophic, rather than textual, bent are more likely to devise more complex descriptions, and some have even pushed for relationality as one of God's primary attributes (e.g., K. Barth, M. Buber), but biblical theology has tended to try to cull the adjectives most inclusive of God's attributes. W. Brueggemann and T. Fretheim are two exceptions. Of course, even while insisting on a god who interpenetrates human beings without coerciveness and with unconditional love, more relational theologians still privilege God in the hierarchy of the divine-human binary, and for the most part privilege man over woman in a dependent hierarchy.

35. Human beings may have indeed brought the flood on themselves (Gen 6), but Fretheim's emphasis on the suffering it caused God seems rather misplaced (21)!

36. Along these lines, J. Plaskow argues that we need metaphors for God that promote divine-human partnership in the ongoing creation of the world, such as

ity, willingness on *both* sides to admit to mistakes and hear the other out.[37] A dialogic theology thus implies the radical notion that sometimes humans can and must be better than God by calling him to account; and it carries the expectation that God will hear and make the necessary adjustments, but without compromising his own integrity (Brueggemann 1997:453). A dogged insistence on divine transcendence may be a theological must, but that does not necessitate a perennially myopic insistence on human culpability. Cannot our sacred texts uphold divine transcendence while at the same time honoring human freedom and agency? In fact, I think that Lamentations goes a long way toward doing exactly that.

A theology that insists on divine omnipotence does little good in today's world; if anything, it is more destructive than constructive, as imperfect humans try to model themselves on the God they *think* they know and understand. It sets up binaries of right and wrong in human relations that further solidify insider and outsider identity constructions, which leads to violence.[38] Recognizing the human inclination toward divinity, L. Irigaray constructs a radical feminist version of a relational god. Such a god would never function to reduce woman to a reflection of man as is the case with all phallocentric systems of knowledge (Irigaray: 62). As such, the attributes of this god are not fixed in a way that precludes genuine reciprocity:

> This God is an ideal whose economy of relations are open to difference, whose internal relations are fluid, unstable, changing, and active, and whose external relation to the human person parallels these same internal dynamics.[39] (Jones: 125)

---

"cocreator" and "companion," rather than hegemonic metaphors like "king" and "lord" (164).

37. I wonder about the viability of insisting that the divine-human relationship is constituted by both relationality *and* asymmetry, as Fretheim does (see Fretheim: 16, 21). Fretheim insists that a theology that privileges relationality "enables truer, deeper encounter and communication; it entails availability and accessibility" (17–18); but is not communication deeply compromised when the relationship is inherently assymetrical, when one party holds all the relevant power? Furthermore, even if we acknowledge that God has the right not to listen to Zion, we can still assert our right to listen to her as ethically motivated readers (I'm grateful to Carolyn Sharp for bringing this nuanced point to my attention).

38. This notion is the cornerstone of R. Schwartz's book.

39. Jones critiques, rightly I think, the utter lack of transcendence in Irigaray's notion of divinity. Because Irigaray is concerned (not wrongly) to avoid reconstituting a hierarchical divine/human relationship (which inevitably leads to the erasure of the "other," traditionally "woman"), she erases the irreducible difference of God, and sees, according to Jones, this "feminine" god as a projection of women's "emerging subjectivity" (138). Jones contends that if Irigaray is so interested in honoring women's genuine difference, God should be granted the same respect (141).

A thoroughly mutable god in this context is not a "bad" god, it is a necessary god. We need a god who models listening and openness to change—a god that evolves as circumstances demand, and allows human existence multiplex manifestations, who facilitates rather than obstructs our growth. And, perhaps most important, we need a god that *never* allows someone to stake a claim of the sort: "God would never do that, or accept that, or love that kind of person."

The beauty of the text that many prize as "sacred" is that it allows dissenting voices into the conversation; it is, then, our responsibility to attend to them. Reading Lam 1–2 intertextually offers us a polyphonic view of truth, as Bakhtin understood it, and that Newsom specifies theologically: "[T]he truth about piety, human suffering, the nature of God, and the moral order of the cosmos can be adequately addressed only by a plurality of unmerged consciousnesses engaging one another in open-ended dialogue" (24). I am not championing a willy-nilly morality based on a "relativistic" god, or god as mere projection.[40] Rather, a fully relational god can be a god that resists reductive pressures, while still forcing us to admit we have no stable moral ground on which to stand, but that *a moral ground is still important and must be carved out of thoughtful and sometimes painful negotiations between parties.* In this arrangement God does not hold the trump card, is no longer the first principle of a logocentric system of knowledge. This arrangement, however, does not constitute a relationship between like and like. In fact, as S. Jones remarks, "[I]f this God is truly to meet humanity in a relationship of mutuality, then this God must also be respected as incommensurably other, as a sign as well as an actual event of

---

40. The reading practices of dialogic biblical theologians should reflect their hermeneutic philosophy—they need to recognize their dialogic relationship with texts, that they author texts as surely as texts "finish" each other. This does not mean that readers should be cavalier about projecting themselves into the texts they are reading, but should, as P. Ricoeur stipulates, engage in a genuine relationship with texts in which texts are allowed to "work" on them as much as they work on texts:

> To understand oneself in front of a text is quite the contrary of projecting oneself and one's own beliefs and prejudices; it is to let the word and its world enlarge the horizon of the understanding which I have of myself. . . . Thus the hermeneutical circle is not repudiated but displaced from a subjectivistic level to an ontological plane. (1998:201)

Ricoeur recognizes that texts do not read themselves and that meaning is always contingent, but he maintains a balance that I think is important to strive for between objectivity and projection. I fully acknowledge that I bring psychological and experiential prejudices to the text that affect the interpretation I end up with, but I am committed to respecting the integrity of the text with the hope of permitting the text to "enlarge the horizon of understanding which I have of myself."

true alterity" (141). So we engage in a balancing act: we must not dismiss God's position as an "event of true alterity" and at the same time must not allow God's otherness to drown human subjectivity.[41]

I am not a systematic theologian, so my job as I see it is to read the text closely, to read closely the god of the text and the divine-human relationship in it, and to demonstrate how it suggests the kind of theology I am outlining here. We need simply to keep reading the text, all of the texts, and foregrounding the dialogic predicament of divine-human interaction each one represents. A dialogic reading strategy of the type illustrated in this book might offer an answer to S. Jones's question of how we can "affirm the otherness and difference of God and persons without reinvoking destructive hierarchies" (140). Such a reading practice would hopefully, over time, reconfigure our theological (and ultimately moral) sensibilities in a more emancipatory direction. If I might venture a utopian vision: Imagine a world in which people are willing to believe that God is in process. If such thinking were to become a part of a new, deeply embedded "master narrative," human self-righteousness might not disappear, but it would lose its divine mandate.

## Marriage as Metaphor

There are many fine linguistic studies on how metaphors function, so there is no need here to rehearse the history of metaphor studies, only to make explicit the understanding of metaphor that will be assumed in this study. A given word is always potentially and at the same time never inherently metaphoric. Metaphors are meaningful only in context.

> [A] word receives a metaphorical meaning in specific contexts, within which it is opposed to other words taken literally. The shift in meaning results primarily from a clash between literal meanings, which excludes the literal use of the word in question and provides clues for finding a new meaning capable of according with the context of the sentence and rendering the sentence meaningful therein. . . . In the statement, "man is a wolf" . . . the principal subject is qualified by one of the features of animal life which belongs to "the lupine system of associated commonplaces." The system of implications operates like a filter or screen; it does not merely select, but also accentuates new aspects of the principal subject.[42] (Ricoeur 1998:197–98)

---

41. Admittedly, the primary goal of this study is to focus on divine relationality rather than transcendence, a necessary first step, I think, toward a dialogic theology that will ultimately reflect the integrity of humanity and divinity.

42. Ricoeur goes on to say, "If . . . we emphasize the role of logical absurdity or the clash between literal meanings within the same context, then we are ready to recognize the genuinely creative character of metaphorical meaning. . . . Logical absurdity creates a situation in which we have the choice of either preserving the literal meaning of the subject and the modifier and hence concluding that the

Metaphors signify through the interaction of "tenor" (principal subject) and "vehicle" (what we think of as *the* metaphor). The tenor is the element the speaker is trying to qualify through the use of a signifier ("vehicle") that can be exploited for the associations it shares with the tenor. In our case, then, Judah/the people equals "tenor" and "adulterous wife" equals vehicle.

While many theories of metaphor have stressed the substitutionary function of metaphors—in which one linguistic unit is substituted for another—I prefer to follow Max Black's emphasis on the *interaction* of the elements of metaphorical expression because it meshes better with my dialogic goals. The interaction between the tenor and vehicle results in a reorganization of the principals of the tenor. "This 'reorganization' is achieved by the vehicle highlighting those qualities in the tenor that are usually associated with the vehicle, while it suppresses those not associated with the vehicle" (9).[43] Everything about the tenor that does not align with the emphases of the vehicle is repressed. In this study, I emphasize those aspects of the people's identity, for example, that are repressed by the vehicle. In other words, there is more to Israel, more to read between the lines than the vehicle allows or wants us to see. If we choose to facilitate a dialogic encounter, or at least to show how the encounter between parties falls short dialogically, we have to read past the inherent manipulative forces of the metaphor. J. Galambush expresses precisely why the interactive understanding of metaphor accords well with a dialogic hermeneutic.

> Max Black's theory of metaphor, which draws attention to the "interaction" of vehicle and tenor so that the vehicle reorganizes our understanding of the tenor, "draws particular attention to the indeterminacy of metaphors, the impossibility of defining with precision what a metaphor "'means.' Because it is not merely two words or two ideas, but two indeterminate *systems* of culturally associated commonplaces that metaphor brings into contact, the precise interaction between tenor and vehicle is to some extent unpredictable and will differ slightly from reader to reader. This indeterminacy is a prime source of the power of metaphor; a metaphor does not make a single statement. . . . (5)

---

entire sentence is absurd, or attributing a new meaning to the modifier so that the sentence as whole makes sense" (1998:199).

43. See also Ricoeur 1998:194–202 for a review of a susbstitionary view of metaphor as opposed to a interactive view: "I entirely agree with the 'interaction view' . . . ; metaphor is more than a simple substitution whereby one word would replace a literal word, which an exhaustive paraphrase could restore to the same place. The algebraic sum of these two operations—substitution by the speaker and restoration by the author or reader—is equal to zero. No new meaning emerges and we learn nothing" (198).

Black's understanding of metaphor takes account of the diachronic, dialogic features of metaphor that emphasize the indeterminacy of meaning. Thus, the marriage metaphor is going to summon different reactions in me than it did in an ancient audience.[44] When I imagine a metaphoric adulterous wife, I do not think necessarily in categories of disobedience, shame, and "pollution," but rather I automatically take into account her free agency, the fact that she might be unhappy, that perhaps her husband does not deserve her loyalty and so forth. Granted, the prophet did not intend that I should consider his metaphor from these angles, but my historical context, saturated with contemporary master narratives, brings associations with it that move against the grain of the original context. In the same way that I can read new meanings into old metaphors, speakers/authors can "activate" aspects of metaphors that have not previously been utilized. Metaphors, through long use, can "die." That is, they become so ingrained in our shared consciousness that they come to be viewed as nearly literal representations of reality rather than metaphorical. For example, the expression "my heart is breaking" is hardly recognized anymore for the metaphor it is. It is probable that ancient Near Eastern cities were so commonly considered female, and often as the wives of patron gods, that no one really thought consciously anymore about what the analogy connoted. Israel's prophets employed this metaphor but with a twist that "reactivated" it. The city is not only a woman and wife, but a deviant and unfaithful one.[45] They chose to activate aspects of the metaphor that were latent and thereby created a fresh and disturbing image of Israelite cities and their inhabitants.[46]

M. Shields, borrowing from B. Lincoln's work on how discourse con-

---

44. A. Labahn makes this point the focus of her study on "Daugher Zion" as metaphor. Although she is primarily interested in how the meaning of this metaphor evolved within biblical contexts, she bases her understanding on the basic principle that "when a text is read in a later time, the sense derived through reading the metaphor changes. Because of new situations, a later reader or hearer of the text generates another sense in his or her interplay with the text, based on individual circumstances" (51).

45. J. Galambush: "Whereas the city-goddesses of the ancient Near East ruled with wisdom and power, in the Hebrew Bible personified cities, almost without exception, are condemned, destroyed, or have their destruction lamented" (26).

46. J. Galambush offers a good example of this process: "If the Lord is my Shepherd . . . , the Lord may feed, carry, chase or chasten me, but he may not kill me and eat me, even though that is one of the things that real shepherds do. If, however, I choose to employ this latent but ordinarily inactive potential, then the familiar metaphor of the Lord as shepherd, which had through long use ceased to be provocative or 'reorienting,' is suddenly new and, in this case, disturbing. This phenomenon of the 'active' and 'inactive' aspects of a metaphor allows for the possibility of a metaphor's expansion by the activation of facets not previously recognized among the 'associated commonplaces' of the vehicle" (7). Galambush

structs societies, notes that discourse, if it is to have a significant impact on society, must be emotionally, not only cognitively persuasive (63). Metaphors, as particularly emotive instances of discourse, have great culture-shaping power. Relational metaphors—marriage, parent-child— naturally tap into deep emotional reservoirs. When a metaphor "fits" just right, in other words speaks to common and intense personal experience, it can cause its associations to appear natural and inevitable, and because of their imagistic, as well as emotional, qualities they tend to be more efficacious than literal speech. For this reason, when they are embedded in oppressive master narratives they contribute to the power dynamics the master narrative is supporting. R. Weems recognizes this process at work in the use to which the prophets put the marriage metaphor.

> Metaphors of power and punishment not only capture the basis of social relations; they naturalize the ideological framework of those relationships. They do this by rendering the power structures and dynamics in those relationships virtually inviolable. (21)

The power dynamics the prophets were interested in inscribing into Israel's psyche had to do with God's unconditional control of his people. The prophets thought the people misunderstood their god and misunderstood what was expected of them, and so they came up with a comparison that no male in Israel could misunderstand—they tapped into the rage and shame every husband would feel if his wife shared herself sexually with other men.[47] And because biblical Israel's sense of itself revolved around the poles of holiness and pollution, of drawing boundaries between itself and "the nations," "sexuality proved . . . to be an apt canvas on which many of the dilemmas that perpetually faced the tiny, struggling nation could be inscribed and represented" (Weems: 70). Strict supervision of women, through marriage and other sexual customs, symbolized tight control of geopolitical boundaries. In my reading, Zion will likewise take advantage of the inherent emotional power of the marriage metaphor, but more implicitly and with different emphases.

## How This Study Will Proceed

The ultimate goal of this study is to provide an example of how we might read biblical texts toward the development of a dialogic theology. Dialogic reading practices highlight the Bible's multiple, conflicting, and complementary voices and thus insist on readings that refuse to privilege one point of view. Breaking the hold of logocentric hermeneutical approaches

---

relies in large part, as do I, on the work of Lakoff and Johnson for her understanding of metaphor.

47. According to E. Siegelman, "an image-laden metaphor that is novel is usually born out of intense feeling: The need to communicate something never communicated in that way before . . ." (6).

provides a strong foundation for unleashing the emancipatory forces inherent in biblical texts. The current social wars raging over biblical interpretations should make it clear that the choices we make about reading have political consequences as significant as those we make in the voting booth or with our checkbook. Our reading practices, in part, construct the symbolic world we inhabit and serve to motivate and justify our actions. Because words, particularly biblical words, possess the power to muster armies, we must approach the text with a certain ethical consciousness. In addition, this influence means that we may start the emancipatory process in the world by showing solidarity with the oppressed of the text.[48]

My dialogic hermeneutic pays close attention to the speech of biblical characters, especially divine speech and human speech that is directed to, or speaks about, God. Chapter 2 focuses on the divine/prophetic discourse that makes a case for Israel/Judah's destruction. I also address the management and evolution of the marriage metaphor from Hosea to Jeremiah to Ezekiel, reading God's words closely for the story they weave about Zion; in other words, I diagnose the architectonics of God's authoring. I examine structure and content to this end. For example, that the woman's words are presented only through indirect discourse in the prophets emerges as an important signifier of YHWH's rhetorical and political goals. And obviously, what YHWH says of her and for her is scrutinized for its ideological agenda. In order to force a dialogic encounter that is not explicit but haunts the background of these texts, I read, in the spirit of midrashic gap-filling, between the lines and hint at a preliminary counterstory for Zion.

Chapter 3 builds on the previous work I have done toward a dialogic reading of biblical laments. One of the main questions asked is: how has the poet of Lam 1–2 altered the basic form of the lament genre to facilitate Zion's need to tell a different story? This chapter also addresses how intertextuality and form-critical concerns coincide with relational/dialogic interpretive practices.

Chapter 4 is the heart of the book. In this chapter, Zion (and I) craft a counterstory that resists the myopic identity in which God and his prophets have confined her. This sounds very close to answering Spivak's question "Can the subaltern speak?" with a "Yes," but at the same time my admission that I am in part crafting this counterstory with her raises some alarms that Spivak and others have addressed. "Even when the subaltern appears to 'speak' there is a real concern as to whether what we are listening to is really a subaltern voice, or whether . . . what is inscribed is not the subaltern's voice but the voice of one's own other" (Griffiths: 27). As Spivak warns, the gendered subaltern, in particular, disappears because

---

48. "This ethics of justice must be extended both to contemporary situations and to the biblical past. It seeks to engender solidarity not just with contemporary wo/men struggling for justice and well-being but also with those whom biblical texts address, argue with, or silence and marginalize" (Schüssler Fiorenza: 12).

she is merely the medium through which competing discourses wrangle for position. In other words, am I hearing Zion's words, or am I speaking for her? Am I just one competing social discourse that is using her for my own purposes? Since her speech is represented only textually, there is no way around interpretive biases, and so I admit that I am putting words in her mouth, many of which an ancient woman approximating Zion's position would surely eschew.[49] In the world of the text, we can assume that Zion's words were crafted by a masculine subject and are laced with hidden and not-so-hidden patriarchal agendas, undermining for some the claims of their liberative potential. So, what am I doing? As a reader, I choose to read the poet's choice of female metaphor against the otherwise patriarchal impulses of the book. I am trying to create a space for a dissenting voice that the Bible itself has permitted into the discourse, but that has rarely been read as the challenge it actually poses to the dominant voice of prophetic ideology. Posing the challenge in gendered terms is simply taking advantage of the terms already set by the biblical authors and animates the discussion for contemporary readers. In short, I have to admit that I am reading first and foremost for myself, although it is my sincere hope that this reading could inspire those whose voices are smothered to assert their own voice against those seemingly insurmountable forces (linguistic and otherwise) that have determined their subjectivity for them.

Chapter 5 consists of a somewhat cursory examination of God's "response" in Second Isaiah to Zion's counterstory. Good intertextual work has been done on Lamentations and Second Isaiah, so I am not as interested in putting them together as I am in reading Lamentations in terms of the earlier prophets. But I do want to play out the dialogic trajectory I started.[50]

Chapter 6 reflects on the theological conclusions suggested by the reading philosophy with which this book has experimented. Since most of the theoretical issues in this regard have already been covered in this introduction, the final chapter focuses on the potential pragmatic results of a dialogic reading of these texts.

---

49. I hope that I am doing what Bloom describes as a "strong misreading," in which "the mighty dead return," but "they return in our colors, and speaking in our voices" (Bloom: 141).

50. Some would argue that the tension introduced in Hosea, Jeremiah, and Ezekiel is resolved in Second Isaiah, but I plan to explore that conclusion in chapter 5 (O'Connor 1999a).

# 2

# The Construction of Daughter Zion
# in the Prophets

*The proper study of mankind is man.* (Alexander Pope, "Essay on Man")

*What is man that the itinerary of his desire creates such a text?* (Gayatri Spivak, "Displacement and the Discourse of Women")

In order to establish to what degree we can read Lam 1–2 as a *response* to the prophetic rhetoric of condemnation aimed at Israel figured as a woman, the "adulterous" wife of YHWH, we need first to look at how the female metaphor is constructed in the prophetic texts. Since my primary aim is to read the relationship between God and the people through the lens of this female figuration, the prophetic texts most in need of deciphering are those that utilize the marriage metaphor as a primary trope for the human/divine relationship. Because several prophetic texts at least allude to this metaphor, it will be useful to narrow down our criteria. The early chapters of Hosea must be included in such a study, if for no other reason than many scholars attribute to Hosea the invention—in an Israelite context—of the husband-wife metaphor.[1] Hosea has few other explicit links to Lam 1–2, but a look at the *ur*-usage of the metaphor will prove helpful for comparative purposes when we move on to texts that have more explicit connections with Lamentations, namely, Jeremiah and Ezekiel.

Recently, scholars interested in tracking the development of the marriage metaphor have offered suggestive evidence for Jeremiah's and Ezekiel's dependence on Hosea's ingenuity.[2] Thus, I start with a fairly cursory examination of how Hosea constructs the identity of the wife-image.

---

1. It is probable that this metaphor has a background in the ancient Near Eastern custom of figuring capital cities as the wife of the patron deity.

2. See, for example, G. Baumann, *Love and Violence: Marriage as Metaphor for the Relationship between YHWH and Israel in the Prophetic Books.*

And because this study is especially interested in aspects of rhetorical dialogism, I pay special attention to the speech of the deity and the use of
quotations as representations of the wife's (and children's) point of view.
These observations lead naturally to theological conclusions and to considerations of the contours of the relationship between YHWH and his wife.
The features of this relationship can then be tracked rhetorically into other
texts that make use of the marriage metaphor. Issues of redaction and
historical context are considered only insofar as they are useful for establishing the rhetorical concerns of the text; for example, it is useful, at some
level, to speak of chronological development from Hosea to Jeremiah to
Lamentations to Second Isaiah (Ezekiel is more difficult to place), or to
note that the events of 587 B.C.E. exert a pressure on the text that opens up
postcolonial reading possibilities.

As I read these texts I pay attention to surface, literal, or "intended"
meanings (i.e., what most would assume the prophet/deity wants us to
read) as well as more submerged signifiers (i.e., what the woman might have
us read if she were given a voice). As C. Exum suggests: "By foregrounding what is repressed, displaced, and undecidable, it draws attention to
the inevitable traces of the woman's point of view in male-authored texts,
traces that subvert the texts' patriarchal authority" (122). Most commentators have opted for the first type of reading, which, following Barthes, has
come to be called "readerly." Sherwood describes a readerly text as a "classic"; it does not "disturb the reader but reinforces her expectations and
gratifies the desire for a unified meaning and narrative closure" (1996:84).
In this type of reading, "images have usually been treated as subordinate
to meaning . . ." (85). Contrary to this emphasis on *what* a text means, I pay
equal attention to *how* it means, how it uses images to control meaning and
manipulate understanding. Asking "how" assumes the text has an agenda,
an assumption that leads to reading suspiciously. How are the binaries
male/female, innocence/guilt, pure/impure, loyalty/disloyalty construed
and normalized? What is omitted in the text's specific semiotic strategy?

Paying attention to images over meaning reveals gaps in the text into
which we can insert a subjectivity for the woman. Reading for the silenced
woman assists us in constructing a dialogic encounter and thus a more
fully realized relationship. At the same time, reading an explicitly monologic text in a dialogic manner highlights just how one-sided the text is as
it stands. It is rife with third-person indicative grammatical constructs of
the type A is B (e.g., the woman is a "whore")—precisely the kind of epistemological statement that deconstruction is meant to challenge. Further,
because the prophetic texts flesh out the contours of many of the Bible's
"master narratives" (or elements of them), reading them with an eye to the
pertinent aspects of the master narrative—patriarchy, covenantal exclusivity, and so on—is necessary in order to establish the extent to which Zion
produces a counterstory in Lam 1–2.

On the theological level, the marriage metaphor was obviously an "important rhetorical tool for defending God's reputation and for addressing Israel's repeated questions about theodicy, suffering, and the inscrutable ways of God" (Weems: 65). But from a socio-rhetorical perspective, the metaphor was an effective device for communicating to the prophet's elite male audience because it played on two issues that mattered to them: (1) a woman who had sexual intercourse outside of her marriage threatened the patrilineal and patriarchal imperatives of unambiguous ancestral lines; and (2) an adulterous wife brought social dishonor to her husband and flouted his inability to control and guard the sexual impulses of the female members of his house, something honorable men were expected to do (Weems:4, 41–43). Thus, the marriage metaphor tapped into Israelite men's deepest anxieties.[3] Concomitantly, it spoke to a need to establish a stable national identity. "[H]uman sexuality repeatedly threatened to undo the fragile myth of kinship and solidarity that defined the nation, forcing the mythmakers to find language and symbols to constrain the nation's contradictory impulses" (Weems: 71). It makes sense that the social chaos Judah was experiencing prior to 587 B.C.E. would result in a metaphor that reflects the need to control chaos on the national level by appealing to the personal. More surprising is the way the master narratives of the elite were turned against them. If the prophets were successful, the audience would be compelled to acquit God of any suspicion of weakness or injustice that resulted in their destruction at the hands of the Assyrians or Babylonians (Weems: 64). Judah's leaders eschewed prophetic rhetoric at the risk of destroying their own master narratives.[4] It is a brilliant ploy. The leadership is compelled to embrace fully their chastisement if they want to maintain their position of power in the status quo. If they protest that their treatment is unjust, then they open the door to those lower on the hierarchical ladder to do the same.

## Hosea 1–3—Establishing the Metaphor

Hosea was apparently a northerner who addressed his revelations to fellow citizens during a particularly tumultuous period, over a period of two decades leading up to the fall of the Northern Kingdom to the Assyrians.

---

3. Situating the metaphor in its cultural context should alert us to the important point that Lakoff and Johnson (*Metaphors We Live By*) made about metaphors—that they are culture dependent and that to understand them, the speaker and addressee must belong to the same cultural world. This is undoubtedly true, but with this study, I am of course more interested in the way these texts have been recontextualized and continue to influence contemporary audiences.

4. "Such a strategy asks men both to identify themselves as the promiscuous woman and to resist that identification" (Shields: 67). A. Bauer also makes this point (55). Further, according to J. Galambush, the entire male population is threatened by their god's loss of power and honor, but according to the metaphor they are responsible for said dishonor (102).

The prophet figures the relationship between God and Israel as a marriage by embodying it as a sign-act—an act in which the prophet lives the experience of the husband-deity by entering into a relationship with a *zonah*, a woman who shames her family through some form of sexual indiscretion:[5] "Go, get yourself a shameless wife and children of shame, for the land will whore away from YHWH" (Hos 1:2). In an honor-and-shame context, a woman's sense of shame is understood as a positive and necessary sentry, overseeing her behavior. In other words, a woman's sense of shame protected her husband's (and family's) honor (Yee 1992:198).[6] Copious amounts of ink have been poured out in an attempt to determine whether the prophet just happened to have such a wife, which was then put to use to illustrate YHWH's sense of betrayal; or whether the prophet took such a wife on the command of the deity; or whether the imagery is purely imaginative. Such an inquiry offers little insight into the rhetorical contours and goals of the text. That the woman is given a personal name, Gomer, may suggest an actual situation, but more to the point of this study, her name provides her a level of subjectivity that will not be sustained when Jeremiah appropriates the metaphor.[7] Essential to the sign-act is that Hosea is rhetorically equivalent with the deity while sinful humanity is rendered female.[8] The theological consequences of this are that the divine is rendered male, while the female is aligned with sin, specifically sinful humanity (Yee 1992:195).[9] While the wife signifies the

---

5. It is unlikely that *zonah* means "whore" or "prostitute" in any literal sense; nor is there any evidence that it points to a "cultic prostitute" (as Hos 4:14 is often translated), or that such an institution ever existed, in either Israelite or Canaanite religious practice. In a context of honor and shame rather, *zonah* refers to a woman that brings shame to her family through her actions. For a recent and fairly substantive review of the traditional scholarly link between Israelite religion and alleged Canaanite sexual cultic practices, see R. Abma (14–20).

6. "The shame of adultery is often understood to adhere to the *man* rather than to the offending woman. . . . In the OT the public shaming (or capital punishment) of the woman transfers the shame onto her, and serves to vindicate the honor of her husband or clan" (Galambush: 30).

7. Of course, on the flipside, this attention to naming only highlights the nearly exclusive power of men to name (Sherwood 1996:299).

8. This suggests a simpler correspondence between tenor and vehicle than is actually the case. As J. Galambush notes, in Hosea 1–3 "the metaphor's tenor is virtually impossible to follow" (44). In other words, "rather than focusing on a single set of people or events and depicting them *through* the metaphoric vehicle of the woman, Hosea focuses on the unfaithful woman and uses this image as the means of addressing the various objects of Yahweh's anger" (Galambush: 51). For the purposes of my study, however, tracing the precise metaphoric path that Hosea sketches is not necessary.

9. This observation evokes L. Irigaray's understanding of God as a victim of phallocentrism, almost as much as woman is: "God is in fact only an imagined screen against which man projects his own identity and thereby secures

people as betrayers of YHWH, the children born of the prophet represent an aspect of YHWH's response to the mother's disloyalty. Signified by divine curses, they reap what their mother has sown.[10] Sherwood notes how YHWH exhibits a "disturbing erasure of paternal feeling" when he names his children with divine curses; and while Gomer may be the shameless mother, she nevertheless continues to have children and obviously suckles and nurtures them through childhood (see Hos 1:8) (1996:141). (It is hard to imagine she has any time to commit adultery while raising three children!) Throughout chapter 1 the prophet reports the words of YHWH as they are spoken to him. In chapter 2, the speech of YHWH and the speech of the prophet are collapsed into one discourse, which is directly addressed to the children (although there seems to be slippage in the addressee, as well, as the chapter continues). The children are commanded to "Contend with your mother, contend! For she is not my wife, and I am not her husband." The children are perhaps being asked to act as witnesses in a divorce proceeding, for the deity/prophet then launches into testimony that supports his dissolution of the marriage; or perhaps they are being asked to intercede with their mother to try to forestall an imminent breach. The former suggests what many readers assume about the use of רִיב, that the text is unequivocally claiming the woman's guilt; the latter leaves open the possibility of YHWH's guilt (from the woman's perspective, at least).

The collapsing of the prophet's marriage into the relationship between YHWH and the people in chapter 2 is where the metaphor gains real force; it is no longer mediated by the image of Hosea and Gomer's marriage. The people are now forced to assume fully the mantle of adulterous woman and thus the punishment attendant upon such a construction: "I will strip her naked, and expose her as in the day she was born; and make her like a wilderness, and turn her into a parched land, and kill her with thirst" (Hos 2:5). While the metaphor still had one foot in reality the children born of the shameful woman were still nonetheless the prophet's, but now YHWH suggests that the children will suffer the mother's punishment because they were born under shameful circumstances: "Upon her children I will have no pity, because they are children of shame" (Hos 2:6). As the metaphor is loosed from its anchor in Hosea's real life, the emotional impact is heightened. Whereas the chapter began with the impression that the deity was attempting to keep some emotional distance between his feelings and those of the prophet, now we feel the full force of YHWH's fury and disillusionment. With the collapse of the emotional wall, the impact on the

---

the perimeters of his own subjectivity" (Jones: 123). This observation of course undercuts patriarchal theology's concern with the irreducibility of their "central principle."

10. Y. Sherwood notes that "the coupling of children and non-love is striking and perverse, and it is reasonable to suggest that it would have appeared so in any society and any historical context" (1996:118).

audience is also profound now there is no distance between themselves and Gomer—while initially they could willingly empathize with Hosea's plight, they are now forced to collude against their own interests.[11]

As YHWH moves more fully into the role of aggrieved husband, we hear the first instance of speech attributed to the wife/mother, in the form of a quotation voiced by God: "For she said, 'I will go after my lovers; they give me my bread and my water, my wool and my flax, my oil and my drink'" (Hos 2:7). This pseudo-dialogism gives the impression that YHWH has attempted to reason with his wife, but that she is belligerent. As support for the accusations in the verse that precedes it, this quote neatly sums up the manner in which she has played the "whore" (זנה) and acted "shamefully" (בוש) (2:6). "Lovers" (from the root אהב) in this context probably alludes to political alliances that the prophet disapproves of, in part because such alliances surely drew Israel's worship to the gods of allies (Keefe: 195). The words that YHWH assigns her suggest a situation of problematic (from the deity's perspective) trade relations, figured as spousal disloyalty. Her words in YHWH's mouth are meant, of course, to buoy YHWH's case against her, but reading deconstructively suggests some slippage in the language. According to YHWH's rendering, the woman goes after lovers because they not only provide her luxury items, but also basic necessities such as bread and water. In this light, her actions do not seem particularly licentious.[12] Grammatically, "lovers" is placed in apposition to a participial form of נתן, suggesting an understanding of the lovers as "providers," not merely ones who give her something happenstance. This implies a situation of grave dishonor and insecurity for the deity. It is the husband's duty to provide for the needs of his wife, a role the text assumes YHWH duly fulfills (Yee 1992:199). The woman's point of view, however, deconstructs the text's assertion that YHWH is the better provider; she has found one superior.

---

11. The audiences' identification is rendered unstable by the movement of the rhetoric. Peggy Day notes the form the initial identification takes: "The respective metaphorical descriptions of Yahweh as magnanimous husband and Jerusalem as ignominious infant and outsider wife serve to reinforce for the intended audience, which was overwhelmingly, if not exclusively, male. Their choice of subject position, as both gender and ethnicity, among other factors, function to unite that audience and compel it to identify with husband Yahweh" (235). See also Y. Sherwood, who notes how the text disrupts its binary hierarchy when men are "audaciously" forced to identify with a promiscuous woman (1996:313).

12. Y. Sherwood reads these quotes as "compliant" with the deity's accusations, which of course they are meant to be (1996:301). Unusually for Sherwood, she chooses not to deconstruct the text's logic in this one place, alluding to the woman as a "puppet of patriarchal rhetoric." But see p. 319, where she discusses the woman's insistence on independence. The idea that Jerusalem is merely attaching herself to the best provider is supported in Jer 44, in which the prophet cites the women as refusing to stop worshiping the Queen of Heaven because it was only when they ceased that they came to "lack everything" (v. 18).

(This notion is supported in Jer 44, which I look at more closely in the next section.) YHWH's anger in Hosea, then, could be read in part as over-compensation, as an attempt to curb the implication that he is as much to blame for her "wanderings" as she is.

> Alongside the picture of a self-assured deity who knows that Israel will return to him, the text presents a jealous and insecure husband who turns to violence in desperation. The tensions of the divine-human metaphor lead to a bizarre situation in which the deity who confidently asserts his superiority is also a rather pathetic figure who lashes out in anger.... (Sherwood 1996:222–23).

In short, even in YHWH's own words, her actions hardly seem deserving of the subsequent punishment. Nevertheless, immediately following the woman's proclamation, YHWH speaks, in adamant grammatical tones, of hedging up her way and blocking her ability to find her lovers. Only then, after he has foiled all her attempts, does he quote her as saying "I will go and return to my first husband, for then I fared better than now" (Hos 2:9). Again, YHWH's own words hint at a relationship in which his patronage is not as desirable as he implies: the woman only chooses to return to him as a last resort and only because he has made it impossible for her to take her preferred route, not because of even a small amount of actual affection or desire, nor the sense that she will be provided for. "[L]ocking her away is not the action of a man assured of his attractive powers, but of a man who realizes that he cannot emotionally captivate his wife, and can only physi-cally capture her" (Sherwood 1996:222–23).

Rather than blatant betrayal, the deity's own words betray Zion's ig-norance: "*She did not know* that I gave her the grain, the wine, and the oil . . ." (Hos 2:10). But perhaps her ignorance constitutes the heft of the di-vine charges against her. Because of her ignorance, YHWH will remove from her the "new grain" and the "new wine"; the wool and linen that covered her will be withheld with the result that her nakedness will be revealed to her lovers (Hos 2:12). In other words, she will be shamed before her al-lies, as she has shamed YHWH.[13] Never mind that her shaming signifies his shame, as well. In a spiteful and seemingly self-defeating move, YHWH will destroy the woman's vines and fig trees, which he claims to have given her but that she believes come from her lovers (2:14). Ironically, his destruction of them can only reinforce her belief that YHWH is not their source as well as affirm her allegiance to other providers.

Thus far, YHWH's tirades seem more the consequence of hurt than anger. He has been passed over for "lovers" that appear to the woman, at least, to be better providers. Of course, opting for a provider who is not her hus-

---

13. "In the OT the public shaming (or capital punishment) of the woman transfers the shame onto her, and serves to vindicate the honor of her husband or clan" (Galambush: 30).

band is reprehensible enough in this social context, but YHWH's accusations fail to convey the dire criminality we can assume was their intent. Negligence and ignorance, perhaps, but a strong case for willful betrayal is not made. The end of chapter 2, with its elaborate reversal of divorce imagery, seems to support this understanding of YHWH's psychology. After having sated his wrath, the deity turns toward reconciliation: "Therefore, I will now allure her, and bring her into the wilderness, and speak tenderly to her" (Hos 2:16). He will return her vineyards, and she will respond to him as she did in her youth. This type of seductive tactic is well-documented as one of the psychological tools of imperial, as well as patriarchal, power: "While the logic of power . . . is fundamentally coercive, its campaign is frequently seductive" (Gandhi: 14). YHWH's ostensibly poignant courting of his estranged wife will apparently succeed in reestablishing their covenant, but only in accord with YHWH's control of her subjectivity. He will put words in and take words from her mouth.[14] She will call him 'ishi ("my man") and not ba'li ("my master"); and he "will remove the names of the Baals from her mouth" (Hos 2:19). In other words, she will no longer choose lovers over YHWH because he will ensure she is incapable of doing so. The chapter and, by implication, the rehearsal of the entire troubled relationship end with a responsorial eschatology—God and all creation co-responding. What began with miscues and appropriated quotations ends in apparent perfect verbal accord. Except . . . the apparent dialogic equality remains entirely a construction of the deity. Even in the final line of the chapter—after reconciliation is so absolute it is rendered in cosmic terms—when YHWH says to Lo-ammi, "You are my people," Lo-ammi does not directly respond, but is reported as saying "[You are] my god" (Hos 2:25c–d).

It is not necessary to say much about chapter 3 except to note that it seems essentially an abbreviated version of chapters 1–2. Like the first two chapters, it juxtaposes punishment and redemption in the form of a metaphor in which the prophet is instructed to love a woman who loves others. Together with chapter 1, it provides a bookend in which the prophet's relationship to a woman is highlighted, whereas in chapter 2, the deity

---

14. G. Baumann comments on the deity's rhetorical disregard for Zion's subjectivity: "Another problematic aspect of the depiction of Israel is that the female figure almost never has a word to speak—and when she does, it is only in supposed quotations that establish her compulsive pursuit of the Baals and make it clear that she lacks any sense of guilt (2:23, 25). The text speaks about her from an exclusively male perspective; her own voice, her own will, even as regards her 'marriage' to YHWH, is not recorded" (125). Similarly, in Bakhtin: "The truth about a man [sic] in the mouths of others, not directed to him dialogically and therefore a second-hand truth, becomes a lie degrading and deadening him, if it touches upon his 'holy of holies,' that is, 'the man in the man.' . . . Truth is unjust when it concerns the depths of someone else's personality" (1984).

becomes more directly one of the subjects of the marriage. Unlike chapter 1, however, chapter 3 is spoken in the first—"YHWH said to me"—rather than third-person singular by the prophet. No quotations are used; the woman is not even provided a name. The allusion to King David suggests the chapter comes from the hand of a later southern editor. In fact, because the chapter adds little rhetorically to what preceded it, it is plausible to suggest the chapter was added with the sole intention of juxtaposing loyalty to God and loyalty to David.

Hosea's bizarre linkages between signifier and signified (e.g., God as a father who kills his own children) create a dissonance in his prophecy that opens the way for deconstructive readings,[15] readings that draw attention to the deity's inconsistencies and allows us to view the situation from the perspective of the woman/wife, thus retrieving for her some subjectivity by not allowing the deity's asserted subject position to stand. Reading for the gaps in the deity's discourse gets trickier in Jeremiah.

## Jeremiah 2–3; 13:20–27

Following the call narrative of chapter 1, Jeremiah begins his preaching, as did Hosea, by figuring the people of Israel as a woman. Chapters 2 and 3 are a collection of separate poems and prose passages, often recognized as having many elements of a רִיב or legal dispute. Although there are a few sections in which feminine imagery gives way to masculine,[16] those that do are held together by the female imagery. Because Jeremiah's prophecies are among the most intensely personal in the prophetic corpus, one might be surprised to find that the prophet did not follow Hosea in depicting his own life in the metaphoric terms assigned to YHWH. This may have to do with the simple fact that Jeremiah's commission presupposes a life of loneliness, without family. In fact, in direct contrast to Hosea's commission, Jeremiah is commanded not to take a wife, or to have children (Jer 16:2).

Chapter 2 begins with the deity speaking directly to the woman, Jerusalem,[17] through the prophet, reminiscing about the early days of their

---

15. Y. Sherwood explores this issue from a semiotics perspective (1996). Sherwood relies on Derrida's definition of "deconstruction" as she understands him, an understanding I support: the primary purpose of deconstructive readings is to "locate the hierarchies that the text is consciously promoting or unconsciously taking for granted" and to interrogate them (174).

16. As K. M. O'Connor notes, the "alternation of addressee between the male and female personae serves to identify the two literary figures as one entity" (1999b:389).

17. The connection between the personification of Jerusalem as a woman and the ancient Near Eastern tradition of city goddesses is commonly accepted. As G. Baumann notes, "The female personification of the city that is found in Zech. 9.9; Isa 1.8; Jer 4:30–31; 6:22–26, and in other places in the Hebrew Bible is,

marriage, when "the bride" loved YHWH (Jer 2:2).[18] The female imagery
is then interrupted by several verses of accusations and threats that do
not require reading through the lens of the marriage metaphor. Feminine
Jerusalem is addressed again in v. 17, in which she is given a lesson in retributive justice: "Have you not brought this upon yourself by forsaking
YHWH your god?" And again in v. 19: "Your wickedness will punish you,
and your backsliding rebuke you." As in Hosea, Jerusalem's wickedness
and backsliding seem connected to her choice of allies and perhaps trading
partners, namely Egypt and Assyria (Jer 2:18). Such anti-"globalism" rhetoric, also featured in Hosea, opens up the text to postcolonial concerns, but
any such effort is confounded by Jeremiah's implicit support of Babylon.
We are left with a group of people struggling over how best to control and
survive imperial pressures. It is a mistake, then, to read Jeremiah's rhetoric
as anticolonial, per se, or uniquely liberative, but rather the orchestration of
positions implied in the text permits us a glimpse into how colonial forces
tear societies apart and channel energy away from community building.
Zion's apparent allegiance to Egypt or Assyria earns the label "idolatrous"
only because the prophet's rhetoric offers divine sanction to a nation that
should otherwise be considered just another colonizer. YHWH's rhetoric
insists he is to be trusted above the people's own choice of imperial allegiance, yet he indicts himself as colluding in the advance of a heinous
colonial oppressor: "For *I am summoning* all the peoples of the kingdom of
the North—declares YHWH" (Jer 1:15).

A new section begins at v. 20 and here the deity quotes the woman for
the first time to bolster his case against her. He accuses her of breaking her
yoke and proclaiming, "I will not serve!" Apparently it is only YHWH she
would not serve because her rebellion consists of making herself available
"on every high hill and under every green tree," images that suggest cultic apostasy. Like Hosea, the religious and political realms intersect in the

---

in terms of religious history, usually traced to the West Semitic tradition of a city
goddess and consort of the city's protecting god; she also bears titles like 'mother,'
'daughter,' and 'virgin'" (68). See also Christl Maier. Contra, however, is R. Abma's stress on the distinction between the marriage metaphors in which the "city"
is personified and those in which the "people" or the "nation" is personified. In
the case of Jer 2, Abma claims that despite the mention of "Jerusalem" in the first
verse, the rest of the context suggests that for Jeremiah, it is the whole nation that
is the tenor for the vehicle of YHWH's "wife." Thus, the assumed reliance on the
ancient Near Eastern tradition of a marriage between a city and the patron deity
does not have any direct influence on Jeremiah's rhetoric. I find her distinction
to be a case of splitting hairs. It seems to me perfectly plausible that the prophets
moved easily between Jerusalem and the people as a whole. Surely, Jerusalem
could be understood as serving a metonymic function for the entire people.

18. Although the distinction is not directly pertinent to this study, K. M.
O'Connor's observation that Hosea's *marriage* metaphor becomes more fully a
"broken *family*" metaphor in Jeremiah is a point well taken (1999b:388).

prophet's rhetoric of accusation. Jeremiah's choice of quotation, however, is much less ambiguous in its rebellious connotations than were Hosea's. As Weems notes, "[W]hereas the wife in Hosea came across as naïve and deceived . . . the woman in Jeremiah lacks innocence" (55). Nevertheless, peering beneath YHWH's tirade exposes a weakness in the deity's case. He himself admits that what she is rebelling against is the yoke YHWH has placed on her.[19] The root (עלל) from which "yoke" derives apparently has typically negative connotations as does its derivative, עֹל. In Jer 27:8, 11, YHWH demands that Israel place itself under the *yoke* of the King of Babylon, an obviously unfortunate comparison; and in the very next chapter, the people are assured that YHWH will break the *yoke* of Babylon from around their necks (Jer 28:2), making clear the negative assessment of bondage rendered in these terms. In Hos 11:4, yoke is contrasted negatively with "bonds of love." And of course, the word is also used in the context of pressing domestic animals into service.

So why does YHWH choose to express his relationship to Jerusalem in such pejorative terms? One is hard-pressed to put a positive spin on the image of YHWH imposing a yoke on the woman, Jerusalem. And likewise, it does not require much empathetic exertion to understand the woman's refusal to serve under these circumstances.[20] God demands loyalty and at the same time makes such a commitment impossible.[21] Furthermore, because *yoke* is frequently employed in situations of vassalage, the audience is motivated to read the link between YHWH and the people through the metaphoric lens of colonialism (see 1 Kgs 12:4, 10 for a domestic version). This may be part and parcel of the ancient Near East's understanding of a woman's role vis-à-vis her husband, but it is nevertheless a particularly harsh expression of that relationship.

As was the case in Hosea, the implication of YHWH's accusations is that the woman's sin is related to her fraternizing with "providers" other than him. In Jeremiah's case, however, there is no suggestion within the texts that utilize the marriage metaphor that such alliances gain her anything of value (Jer 2:18), but rather it is (unintentionally) hinted that her rebellion is provoked by the oppressive demands of YHWH. Outside of the metaphor's

---

19. Some, including Abma, read with the *qethib* "I broke" (שברתי), against the LXX (217). The pronominal suffix can be read as an archaic second-person feminine singular form as seems to occur a number of times in this text. The ambiguity, however, is interesting in itself.

20. Note also Jer 2:31, in which YHWH quotes the people as proclaiming "We are free; we will come to you no more!" As N. Lee observes of this verse, the people are not in any sense lamenting a life without YHWH; in fact, they prefer it (110).

21. Francis Landy notes how the ambiguity of metaphors in Hosea sets up a double-bind for the people—they must love God, but such a demand "is rendered hateful by its impossibility" (39). This holds true for Jeremiah, too.

rhetorical influence, however, there is a text that can illuminate the wife's side of things. Jeremiah 44:15–19 states in unequivocal terms that there is much to be gained by rebelling against YHWH.[22] Interestingly, the (probably Deuteronomistic) author does not bother to phrase the people's point of view in the mouth of the deity or the prophet as is usually the case, but lets them speak their own words in direct discourse, and what they say compels sympathy: "[W]e will do everything we have vowed—to make offerings to the Queen of Heaven and to pour libations to her, as we used to do.... For then we had plenty to eat, we were well off, and suffered no misfortune. But since we stopped making offering to the Queen of Heaven and pouring libations to her, we have lacked everything . . ." (Jer 44:17–18). As with the Hosean texts, we are again confronted with the disquieting evidence that YHWH simply is not the provider he demands to be worshiped as.[23]

In any case, returning to the metaphor, the woman's fraternizing renders her unclean, making her an unfit companion for YHWH, ritually or otherwise. In the second use of indirect discourse—"How can you say, 'I am not unclean (טמא), I have not gone after the Baals' "? (Jer 2:23)—we have the deity's report of her denial of the charge. There is a disconnect between this alleged denial and what the deity reports of her in the next quotation, in which she boldly claims her allegiance to her lovers: "It is hopeless, for I have loved strangers, and after them I will go" (Jer 2:25). Perhaps she is compelled to make this admission because between the two quotes, YHWH offers passionate testimony concerning her apostasy. He compares her to instinct-driven animals in heat, happy to appease the sexual appetites of all comers (Jer 2:23–24). The animalization of the woman is unique, not even repeated "in the most enthusiastic pornographic descriptions of Ezekiel 16 and 23" (Brenner: 93). Reading her quote as it is typically translated suggests some despair on her part over her situation (the root יאש does not seem to lend itself to flip usage), as if she is distressed by her own actions, but cannot control them. In any case the construction of the entire second half of v. 25 is ambiguous and leaves open several interpretive possibilities. Following Isa 57:10, in which the same three roots are used in a slightly different configuration, we may read here: "You did *not* say, 'It is hopeless' "; or possibly, "You said, 'It is *not* hopeless (or desperate).' " It seems unlikely that YHWH would attribute to the woman any sense of shame or mitigate her guilt otherwise by having her admit that her situation is desperate and out of her control to some degree. The most logical translation seems the last one: after YHWH's searing portrayal of her as a being constituted solely by lust, it makes sense to read her (at least in his construction) as proclaim-

---

22. I am indebted to my colleagues in the Lenox Colloquium for the observation that this text provides leverage for my reading.

23. Jeremiah 44 directly contradicts YHWH's assertion in Hos 2:9, which I looked at in the previous section.

ing that despite his assessment of her not all is lost—she has strangers that will love her if YHWH will not. In other words, he reads her as cavalierly disregarding her shameful conduct, and in fact quite willing to compound it. The LXX rendering of this verse may support this conclusion: "but she said, 'I will act manly,' for she loved strangers, and went after them." It's difficult to get a clear sense of what ανδριομαι means in this context, but its play on gender is provocative: In a context in which women are equated with sinful behavior, the implication is that the characteristics that YHWH most detests in her mirror typical male behavior.[24] At the least, the LXX version suggests a shamelessness on the woman's part. Reading between the lines, however, suggests an attitude not so different from what we inferred in Hosea—what she cannot get from YHWH, she will (understandably) search out elsewhere.

The insinuation that YHWH might bear a portion of the blame for the actions of his people is given additional support in v. 29. Although this verse occurs in a long passage that is not explicitly directed at the woman, it is directed toward the people as a whole and has some bearing on my reading. After snidely telling the people that they should look to one of their many other gods, rather than to him, to save them, YHWH asks rhetorically, "Why do you bring suit (ריב) against me? You have all rebelled against me!" What lies behind this situation is probably a ritual lamentation performed by the people, whereby the people make supplication to YHWH in an attempt to avert the looming crisis.[25] We can infer from YHWH's quote that the people hold him accountable for what has befallen them, but YHWH retorts that they, not he, are to blame. The relationship seems to have degenerated into a childish blame game, with YHWH holding all the cards. YHWH feels betrayed by the people's lack of sole allegiance to him, but the people apparently still feel justified in expecting him to act as their god and to rescue them.[26] Ironically, this text suggests that the people might be surprised to discover that they are requesting YHWH to save them from himself: "In vain I have struck down your children" (Jer 2:30). The dissolution of the relationship seems to be solely a condition of YHWH's assessment of it. Some portion of the people, at least, seem to think that the covenant is intact. The prophet's assessment to the contrary may be, in part, a tendentious theodic strategy. The notion that Israel's suffering is the result of YHWH's justified punishment is a common exilic and postexilic response to what otherwise could be construed as YHWH's impotence.

---

24. There is no indication that ανδριομαι carries any negative connotation. To the contrary, it seems typically to indicate a quality of courage; but perhaps in the mouth of a woman it would be heard as arrogance, or inappropriate boundary crossing.

25. In another study, I suggest that lament psalms be read as sanctioned lawsuits against the deity (2002).

26. See also the people quoted in Jer 8:19bc.

At Jer 2:33, through the end of the chapter, the voicing switches back to addressing a female object and increases in vitriol. According to YHWH, Wife Judah is so adept at procuring her lovers that she even teaches women already practiced in evil a trick or two. YHWH's accusations shift from adultery/idolatry to social sins when he indicts her for shedding the blood of the innocent poor (Jer 2:34). This adulteress par excellence and heartless murderess has the nerve, according to YHWH's rendition of her defense, to audaciously assert that "I am innocent; surely his anger has turned from me" (Jer 2:35a). This claim, more than anything else, seems to enrage the deity: "Take note! I will bring you to judgment for saying 'I have not sinned'!" (Jer 2:35b). Again, if we choose to read against the text and from her perspective, we can infer a genuine expectation that YHWH has no reason to be angry with her. It is a message similar to that found in lament psalms—the supplicant claims or implies that the affliction she is suffering (often at the hands of YHWH or because of his neglect) is baseless, hence the request that YHWH act justly by bringing deserved relief.[27] Getting specific, YHWH states that her "lover," Egypt, will shame her, as did her previous lover, Assyria (Jer 2:36). Stepping outside the metaphor for a moment, we can surmise that, according to the prophet, Israel has simply made poor political choices (i.e., she has chosen the *wrong* lovers). Apparently, Babylon would have been a more acceptable choice (see Jer 27:8–11).

Chapter 3 rehearses many of the same themes as chapter 2, but one interesting aspect of the chapter noted by M. Shields is that, in Jer 3:1–4:4, "the move from accusation to promise . . . is mirrored by a move from female imagery to male imagery," the result of which is the reinforcement of the equation between women and sin, a powerful symbol of women's marginality (1995:68–71). Much of Jer 3 is about boundary transgression. A marriage metaphor is one of the best ways in a patriarchal society to transmit a message about social boundaries:

> The use of gender-specific language is a particularly powerful way to indicate the breaking of boundaries in a patriarchal context, such as the Bible. In the patriarchal symbolic world, where the self is defined as male, the primary image of the "other," that which is not self, is woman.... [I]t is thus the very marginality of women, their place at the boundaries of patriarchal society, which makes the imagery work so well. (Shields 1995:66)

According to this rhetoric, Zion can be fully herself only within the parameters established by patriarchy, under the control of a man. In other words, adulterous Jerusalem is not what she once was or should be, so she is "not."

---

27. Many commentators read the lament psalms as prayers of contrition, but in fact very few live up to that description (see my *God in the Dock*). Even the church's so-called penitential psalms are hardly penitential.

Before saying more on this, let us look at the only quotation of the woman in the chapter. The opening parable of chapter 3 gives the impression that the chances for reconciliation are slim to none: "If a man divorces his wife, and she leaves him and marries another man, can he ever go back to her?" (Jer 3:1). According to Israelite law, once a marriage is dissolved and the woman marries someone else, she cannot remarry her first husband. As YHWH puts it, in such a case, "Would not the land be defiled?" (Jer 3:1). Apparently, this situation comes too close to adultery, and the requirements of patrilineage would become confused, as well (which, of course, is one of the primary issues surrounding adultery). After yet another rehearsal of her adulterous crimes (Jer 3:2), YHWH cites her as crying out to him when the rains did not come: "Father! You are the companion of my youth. Can one hate and rage for all time?" (Jer 3:4–5a). This short passage has many of the elements of a typical lament psalm: complaint; reference to past relationship; question about how long YHWH will allow the suffering to continue. Once again, there is no acknowledgment of guilt on the woman's part, and more important in terms of the deity's accusations, there is no indication of a refusal to be in relationship with YHWH. The woman is crying out to God in standard Israelite ritual lament fashion and in fact seems passionately committed to YHWH, addressing him with a paternal endearment. But YHWH chooses to read this cry as shameless disregard for her adulterous/idolatrous activities: "You had the forehead of a whore; you refused to be ashamed. Just now you called to me . . ." (Jer 3:3b–4a). Although the final line of this section is uncertain (Jer 3:5b: ותעשי הרעות ותוכל), YHWH seems to be saying that she "has had her cake and eaten it, too." In other words, she goes after her lovers and yet expects to be accepted when she turns to him for help. Rather, basic psychology suggests a severe case of overcompensation—YHWH blames her for his inability to protect her.

Following a (probably Deuteronomic) prose interlude that promises reconciliation between God and his people and the reunification of the north and south, the chapter ends with one last divine lament over the infidelity of the House of Israel *cum* faithless wife, followed by the people (now addressed as YHWH's children) proclaiming their intention to return to their God. The people's intent is conveyed this time not by an indirect quote, but directly. Significantly, they speak without any grammatical mediation:

> Behold, we are coming to you,
> for you are YHWH our God.
> Truly the hills are a delusion,
> the orgies on the mountains.
> Truly in YHWH our God
> is the salvation of Israel. (Jer 3:22b–23)

What the text refuses to offer to the woman—her own voice—it offers to her (male) children. With that, "monologue becomes dialogue and chastised hope emerges" (O'Connor 2001:492).[28] Perhaps, but it is not a hope equally available to the woman. Only males are the recipients of God's promises: "Turn back, rebellious children; I will heal your afflictions" (Jer 3:22a). Underlying the metaphor, then, is the suggestion that repentant Israel gets to resume its status as a collective of males and will no longer have to identify its subjectivity with femaleness. "[O]nce they have identified with and rejected the negative female metaphors, they return to the comfortable subject position of sons to God's father in the patriarchal symbolic order" (Shields 1995:71). The result for women, however, is that they are left with a sinful identity or none at all. This holds not only for the woman of the text, but for living women as well. M. Shields discusses C. Newsom's idea that "any symbolic thinking which uses a specific group of people cannot simply be symbolic—it also has an implication for the behavior of that group of people" (Shields 1995:72; Newsom 1997:155). Shields goes on to say that "although the discourse is disguised as neutral . . . it acts ideologically to exert pressure on the woman to be a faithful wife, mother and daughter, the only positive roles allotted to her within the boundaries created by patriarchy" (Shields 1995:72).

Chapter 13 includes one short passage that is worth looking at because it features another instance in which YHWH quotes the woman in the context of condemning her behavior. Again, although the Hebrew is not clear, poor choice of allies seems to be the issue, couched in the image of adultery: "What will you say when they appoint as head over you those you trained as chiefs among you?" (Jer 13:21). According to YHWH, one thing she might say is: "Why have these things come upon me?" (Jer 13:22). YHWH is quick to explain, "it is for the greatness of your sins that your skirts are lifted up, that you are sodomized [lit., your backside/buttocks treated violently]" (Jer 13:22). Taking YHWH's account of her question at face value, we may surmise that the bewilderment it expresses is as likely genuine as not. Once again, reading on multiple levels raises at least a question about Woman Judah's guilt. Here, either she is extraordinarily and persistently insolent, or is experiencing a sincere disconnect between her self-understanding and her affliction. Certainly, the truth is more complex, but insofar as the latter is the case, then what YHWH says next can only increase the dissonance. Not only must she suffer the pain and indignity of rape, but she is made to understand that it is YHWH himself who commits the act: "I myself (אני וגם) will lift up your skirts over your face, and your disgrace will be seen" (Jer 13:26). It is hard to ignore the (violent) homoerotic connotations in this text, connotations that force us to consider the text's colonial context. God rhetorically feminizes the male elite of Judah and proceeds to sexually violate them. In colonial contexts, such as India under Great Britain, the indigenous males were often discursively constructed as effeminate

---

28. O'Connor reads the children as the exiled Judeans, the implied audience of the prophetic words.

in contrast to the robust masculinity of British males. In the context of the ancient Near East, there is evidence that conquered males were anally penetrated by their conquerors as a way of shaming them and signifying the victors' virility and military superiority. As such, it is plausible that the male elite who were the audience for the prophet's oracles would have made the connection between this practice and YHWH's threats. Taken as a response to the appeals Zion apparently has been making to YHWH (see Jer 3:4–5), his violent actions would be beyond bearing. But in terms of theodic logic, it at least explains why YHWH would not respond positively to her appeals—her "whorings" have left him no option but to respond in the manner he has (Jer 13:27).[29]

As a last point to round out my observations, Jer 31, which functions as a divine proclamation of reconciliation, contains a number of female figurations that do not include violence. Notable, however, is the absence of the wife metaphor in this context. Israel as young woman, daughter, and mother predominate. While overtures to peace and conciliatory rhetoric are welcome, it should be noted that the "wife" is not included in the "new covenant" (Jer 31:33).[30] Perhaps only desexualized women can be tolerated in YHWH's new vision?[31]

Hosea's use of the marriage metaphor juxtaposes condemnation with hope and reconciliation. The god of Hosea seems hurt, sad, and jealous. What hope there is in Jeremiah appears as an afterthought, and his god seems wrathful and vengeful. Where the two prophets agree is in their treatment of the woman's subjectivity—the only subjectivity either of them allow her is what we can manage to read between the lines of their accusations and ostensible quotations. Hosea at least provides her a name; Jeremiah does not bother. What both do give us is the opportunity to hear her voice, however veiled and mediated. Ezekiel is not so generous.

## Ezekiel 16 and 23

Ezekiel 16 is a long chapter and for our purposes the more important of the two we will examine since in it YHWH addresses Woman Jerusalem directly, in second-person feminine singular speech. One obvious way in which Ezekiel differs from Hosea and Jeremiah in its use of the marriage metaphor is that it couches its speech to the woman in a more discursive

---

29. It is interesting that the prophet is cast in both a censorious role and that of victim. In 20:7, Jeremiah accuses God of raping him, thus casting himself in the role of censured Jerusalem. Perhaps this served to some extent as an inspiration for the speech of Zion in Lam 1–2.

30. In Ezek 25–39, the promises of restoration are devoid of references to the feminized city (Galambush: 3).

31. See A. Brenner for some discussion of chapter 31 and its relation to the marriage metaphor (97–98).

fashion and with a sustained narrative.[32] In fact, we are treated to a long narrative recounting of YHWH's betrothal and marriage to Jerusalem, from her youth to her downfall. This narrative of their relationship offers an unusually deep and systematic account of YHWH's perceptions of his wife's behavior. Every word spoken is unequivocally from his mouth (mediated through the prophet, of course). Jerusalem is never quoted, directly or indirectly. The speech of the chapter is presented in I-you language that "constitutes Yahweh as subject and the child/woman Jerusalem as object" (Shields 1998:7). Unlike Hosea and Jeremiah, there are no complicated variations in speaking subject or addressee. For these reasons, the metaphor takes on a visceral power it lacks in Hosea and Jeremiah, but differences in structure and intensity cannot account fully for the outrageously offensive impression conveyed by Ezek 16 and 23. I believe that Galambush is correct that "a key element in Ezekiel's uniquely visceral rendering of the marriage metaphor is his focus on the woman and especially on the female body as both defiled and defiling. . . . [T]he insistent focus on the bloody pollution of Jerusalem's body is distinctive to Ezekiel" (102).[33] Because for Ezekiel the feminized city metaphor implies a feminized temple, the bloodiness (hence uncleanness) of the female body, both through natural processes (birth and menstruation) and in this case "unnatural" processes (infanticide), offers a compelling explanation for the necessity of YHWH's abandonment of his temple—an explanation toward which the entire book of Ezekiel is striving.

> Given Ezekiel's sensitivity to the symbolic connection between the womb of Yahweh's wife and the inner sanctum of Yahweh's temple, his graphic depiction of a Jerusalem polluted from within by unclean blood has disastrous implications. At the level of the vehicle, Yahweh's wife is unclean in both her behavior (adultery) and her substance. Intercourse, the penetration of her unclean body, would be an abomination, even if performed by a (merely) clean male; such contact between the Holy One and a bloody woman would be unthinkable. (Galambush: 104)

Furthermore, at the level of the tenor, the temple has become uninhabitable for the deity because of its blood defilement.[34]

Chapter 16 begins at the beginning, with Jerusalem's birth to Canaan-

---

32. J. Galambush notes that while Hosea and Jeremiah use the marriage metaphor in a more "impressionistic" fashion, Ezekiel's use of the metaphor is marked by "conceptual coherence" (78–81).

33. She also notes that Ezek 16 is the only use of the marriage metaphor banned by the rabbis (*Meg.* 4:10) for liturgical use.

34. As she explains, "[T]he marriage metaphor is especially suited to depict the defilement of Yahweh's temple. If the city is a woman, then the temple is her vagina, and the offense of Jerusalem's granting illicit 'access' to foreign men and competing gods becomes plain, both as a legal transgression and as a personal injury to the husband" (87).

ite parents, her mother an Amorite and father a Hittite. For the priestly Ezekiel, her origins already mark her as unclean. Unlike her portrayal in the previous prophets we examined, here the woman is genetically flawed and carries with her the constant threat of defilement. Her actions, in effect, merely constitute a later reflection of her core being/identity. From her birth she is abhorred, abandoned to die by her own people. YHWH finds her naked, wallowing in her birth blood, and generously wills that she should live. When she reaches puberty, he betroths himself to her, consummating their relationship sexually and covenantally, so that she becomes his possession (Ezek 16:8) (Baumann: 59).[35] He rescues her from the shame of her nakedness by clothing her extravagantly, in fabrics reminiscent of those used for the tabernacle and the tent of meeting, which highlights Ezekiel's concern that the tenor of the metaphor be understood more specifically as the temple rather than merely the people, or the land. Because of YHWH's tender and doting spousal care, Jerusalem grows into abundant and beautiful womanhood. In this scenario, YHWH plays "Henry Higgins" to his "Eliza Doolittle," a trope that suggests yet again a connection between patriarchal and imperial power dynamics. The task of "civilizing" the "barbaric" peoples is a common justification for colonialism (Berquist: 24). The idea that "the colonies require the civilization of the empire for their own protection" is another way imperial power is legitimated. Without God's graciousness and protection, she would have perished. Her fame spreads because of her divinely conferred beauty, which is "perfect because of my splendor that I bestowed on you, says YHWH God" (Ezek 16:14).

Verse 15 marks the end of the honeymoon. The woman has apparently thrived under YHWH's care, but we are not given the slightest window onto her inner thoughts. What we might expect her to say could well resonate with the self-other experience of Hegel's master-slave dialectic—a concept put to emancipatory use by postcolonialists—as Sartre conceives it: "I am possessed by the Other; the Other's look fashions my body in its nakedness, causes it to be born, sculptures it, produces it as it is, sees it as I shall never see it. The Other holds a secret—the secret of what I am" (Sartre: 209). In this scheme the slave is a subject without subjectivity. Likewise Daughter Zion: "There is . . . no sense of an individual personality here. She is entirely what Yahweh has made of her," (Shields 1998:13). The prophet gives us no access to the woman's thoughts or words. What we are told is that she misuses the gifts of beauty that YHWH bestowed upon her: "But you played the whore because of your fame, and lavished your whorings on any passer-by." The root זנה, which appears twice in this verse, is used for the first time. It will be used many more times throughout the chapter, as a verb, a noun, and an appellation, referring to the woman and her deeds.

---

35. In Ezek 16:8 there is a direct connection between marriage and covenant (*berit*), unlike in Jeremiah, who does not seem to make any semantic connection between the two.

Ezekiel carefully constructs Jerusalem as a *zonah*, a "whore" (i.e., shameless or sexually deviant woman). In fact, after calling her "Jerusalem" at the start of the chapter, he never refers to her again by any name other than "you," "whore," or "adulterous wife." By contrast, the use of *zonah* by Hosea and Jeremiah was notably spare.

One of YHWH's primary complaints is that Jerusalem transforms the bounteous gifts he has lavished on her—silver and gold; fine fabrics; choice flour, honey, and oil (Ezek 16:10–13)—into means of paying homage to other gods/lovers (Ezek 16:17–19). In other words, the clothes of honor with which he bedecked her, she takes off, to her (and more importantly, his) shame. He also accuses her of the crime of infanticide, a crime that is either only hinted at or nonexistent in Hos 1–2 and Jer 2–3, 13. She allegedly offers the children that she bore to YHWH as sacrifices to her lovers/idols. He emphasizes this crime by stating it once, and then again a verse later: "As if your whorings were not enough! You slaughtered my children and delivered them up as an offering to them" (Ezek 16:20b–21). The image of mothers sacrificing their children adds to the perverse portrait being painted of the woman.

> At the level of the tenor, literal *fathers* would in fact have offered their children as sacrifices. The metaphorical transfer of the act to "mother" increases the horror of the act in several ways. First, the image works against the commonplace of mother as a nurturer. Second the metaphor depicts the mother usurping the prerogative of the father; the woman is taking the fruits of her sexual obligation to her husband and transferring them to idols, who as "lovers" at the level of the vehicle, are the husband's sexual competitors. (Galambush: 84)

When all is said and done, what her "abominations and whorings" add up to is a failure to "remember the days of [her] youth, when [she was] naked and bare, flailing about in [her] blood" (Ezek 16:22), from which YHWH rescued her. In other words, she bestows her cultic allegiance on undeserving parties.

The deity's accusations get more specific in the next section (Ezek 16:23–29). The passers-by to whom the woman offers herself are specified as the Egyptians (her "lustful neighbors"), the Assyrians, and the Babylonians. With Hosea, we discussed the possibility that her attentions to these "lovers" might be motivated in part by their ability to provide for her. In Jeremiah, that is a harder position to defend, although not out of the question. In Ezekiel's portrayal of her, it is an altogether untenable thesis. Her fraternization is only a mark of her utter depravity: "You whored with the Assyrians because of your insatiable lust; you played the whore with them and still you were not sated" (Ezek 16:28). As A. Brenner notes, in the context of the prophetic adulterous woman metaphor, female sexuality cannot have a legitimate motivation, and the woman is stripped of selfhood: "The metaphorized female creature is motivated by neither love nor by any other acceptable human-social convention. She/it is motivated by lust" (Brenner: 92). Underneath the sexual rhetoric of contempt can still be found allusions to the actual crimes from the prophet's perspective. As was intimated in Hosea and Jeremiah, a political-economic reality underlies the metaphor of whoring. Babylon, with whom she "excessively whored," is referred to as the "land of merchants" (Ezek 16:29). As we observed in Hosea and Jeremiah, those with whom she has whored are likely those with whom she has traded and made political alliances. Egypt, Assyria, and Babylon were all, in their time, either enlisted by or forced themselves upon Judah as allies and overlords. To compound her guilt in YHWH's eyes, Jerusalem, the whore, pays her suitors to fornicate with her (Ezek 16:31–34). It is in this context that he specifically calls her "wife of adultery"; and this lack of pragmatism in his wife's behavior seems to incense him. Rather than being solicited like most whores, she seeks out her lovers and in her desperation pays them.

The chapter moves from a recital of the couple's early history, to a general description of the wife's crimes, to more specific accusations, to finally reach a rhetorical crescendo in the middle part of the chapter. Starting at v. 35, YHWH's vitriol reaches its peak: "Therefore, whore, hear the word of YHWH! . . . I will gather all your lovers . . . against you from all around and . . . [t]hey shall gang rape you and . . . stone you and sever you up the middle with their swords" (Ezek 16:35–40).[36] Any identity she may have attempted to construct apart from YHWH's control is violently eradicated (Shields 1998:13). YHWH makes the claim that these punishments are in accord with Israelite law (Ezek 16:38). Deuteronomy 22:22–24 does indeed sanction the stoning of women caught in adultery, but the man with whom she is caught and against whom the law is actually directed is to be stoned alongside the woman. In Ezekiel, not only does the rhetoric exceed the demands of the law, but, in general, only female sexuality is figured as offensive; the rapists are only tools in YHWH's retributive scheme. What G. Baumann says about the portrayal of sexuality in Jeremiah is equally true in Ezekiel and anywhere the marriage metaphor is deployed in a punitive context: "Male sexuality . . . is criticized only in individual men (Jer 5:7–8), but its real-life character does not become the vehicle of imagery for divine punishment. Since male sexuality is present in YHWH, who uses it as sexual violence, it acquires on the one hand a strongly violent aspect, and on the other a positive connotation: it appears as the good and right kind of sexuality" (124). Even its violent aspects are construed as "good and right." The denouement of this section is disturbingly dissonant. After

---

36. R. Weems notes that Ezekiel's "lurid descriptions are so candid and protracted they threaten to blur the boundaries between preaching and raving" (60). See J. Galambush for an explanation of בתק as a reference to violent phallic penetration (71 n. ee).

this orgy of blood, the deity claims: "Then I will have sated my fury against you, and my jealousy shall turn away from you; I will be calm, and will be angry no more" (Ezek 16:42). The entire scene is reminiscent of a low-budget psycho-slasher movie. In Ezekiel's vision, the deity, with his wild mood swings and blood lust, seems nearly psychopathic.

In spite of his ostensibly becalmed demeanor, however, YHWH immediately returns to condemnatory rhetoric in the next section: "Have you not committed depravity beyond all your abominations?" (Ezek 16:43b). The section from 16:43–52 adds little of significance to the portrait already painted of Woman Jerusalem, except to recount her crimes—this time using a sibling metaphor. Judah (who is not named in the entire section) is compared to her "sisters" Samaria and Sodom, both previously condemned for their abominations and haughtiness. But Jerusalem is told "you have made your sisters appear righteous by all the abominations that you have committed" and that "you have brought about for your sisters a more favorable judgment" (Ezek 16:51–52). The section and chapter end on a word of hope. Perhaps because Jerusalem has mitigated the guilt of her sisters, YHWH "will restore their fortunes" (Ezek 16:53). But then he will restore Jerusalem along with them, seemingly in order that she feel her shame more acutely in contrast to their lesser crimes (Ezek 16:53b–54).

Finally, although Jerusalem has broken the covenant with YHWH (16:59), he will remember the covenant and establish an everlasting one (Ezek 16:60). Reminiscent of the concluding section of hope in Hosea (though lacking in Hosea's tenderness),[37] Ezekiel's God will reestablish a relationship with the woman. But even the rhetoric of reconciliation leaves the woman devoid of subjectivity and the text of dialogism—it is not for anything she has done or could do that he reconciles with her; it is only because he remembers the covenant and chooses to forgive her (Weems: 63).[38] He will establish his covenant with her, and she will, simply, know that he is YHWH. His forgiveness will cause her to remember her crimes and feel shame; and like the wife in Hosea she will be silenced forever (Ezek 16:62–63). Rhetorically, her silencing is projected into the future, but in fact is already accomplished in the text. More than Hosea or Jeremiah, each of which to a greater or lesser degree shares the goal of denying the woman any subjectivity, Ezekiel has systematically stripped all traces of speech from her. In other words, Ezekiel is monologic in the extreme. A singular perspective is presented and assiduously guarded from any incursions between its lines. The preceding exegesis is a case in point—try as one might

---

37. R. Weems reads this section of Ezekiel as "acrid" and little more than a "parenthetical aside" (63).

38. J. Galambush correctly points out that the promise of restoration is never actually realized for the woman in Ezekiel. In Ezek 40–48, the chapters of reconciliation, the elimination of the feminine metaphor is apparently a precondition for the restoration of the temple (125).

to get beneath the surface of the rhetoric, the exegete is hard-pressed to find the woman's point of view lurking anywhere in the text. This demonstrates how the denial of speech—even if only in the form of direct or indirect speech, makes nearly impossible the recovery of any subjectivity for the woman.

My last task in this chapter is to scan Ezek 23 for any additional information to contribute to our quest of determining the features of the prophets' construction of the woman figured as YHWH's wife. The voicing of chapter 23 switches back and forth between second-person and third-person feminine singular address. The chapter begins with the deity speaking only to the prophet about two sisters, both of whom became YHWH's wives after their time as prostitutes in the land of Egypt, and both of whom eventually betrayed him. Echoing the structure of chapter 16, chapter 23 begins with a recital of the women's early history, but this time their story begins in Egypt, where "their breasts were caressed and their virgin bosoms fondled" (Ezek 23:3). It may be worth noting that in both chapters 16 and 23, YHWH (like Hosea) knowingly marries women of questionable repute. Rhetorically speaking, it may call his motives into question. The women are given names in this chapter, Oholah ("her tent") and Oholibah ("my tent is in her"), referring to Samaria and Jerusalem, respectively. Oholah's history of whoring after the Assyrians and subsequent punishment by YHWH through those same lovers is related primarily to set up a contrast with Oholibah. The prophet's attention to the women's relations with Israel's superpower neighbors supports Kwok's contention that Ezek 16 and 23

> must be situated in the context of colonial relations between Israel and Judah and the foreign powers, which led eventually to the conquest and exile of the elites. . . . In the text, the woman was used as a trope for the land and the nation, and sexual images became tropes for colonial dominance. Ezekiel subscribes to the patriarchal ideology of gender and depicts Judah and Israel as feminine, the subjugated colonial subjects, while the foreign aggressors are hypermasculine.[39] (Kwok: 81)

But the prophet does not resist the imagery of the foreign nations overpowering his nation—in fact, he condones it. It is precisely this coalescence of power and ideology that positions God as a colonial overlord in these texts. YHWH could not, after all, be aligned with the effeminacy of his own people.

As chapter 16 already alluded to, Oholibah's lustful whoring is worse than her sister's (Ezek 23:11). Where Oholah shared her bed with only the Assyrians, Oholibah extended her favors to the Babylonians, as well. She is charged with being too easily taken in by the Assyrians' and Babylonians' good looks and authoritative stature, which rouses her uncontrollable lust (Ezek 23:14–16). After sating her desires, she turns from her Babylonian

---

39. G. Yee makes a similar point in her discussion of Ezekiel (2003:111–34).

lover in disgust (probably an allusion to Jehoiakim's rebellion against Nebuchadnezzar—2 Kgs 24:1), just as YHWH turns from her in disgust (Ezek 23:18). Chapter 23, with its focus on Jerusalem's sexual activities, is a degree less violent than chapter 16, but its voyeurism and graphic descriptions of sexual organs imbues it with a lewdness unmatched even by chapter 16:

> Yet she increased her whoring,
> remembering the days of her youth,
> when she played the whore in the land of Egypt,
> and lusted after her lovers there,
> whose genitalia were like those of donkeys,
> and whose organs[40] were like those of stallions.
> Thus you longed for the depravity of your youth,
> when the Egyptians fondled your bosom
> and caressed your young breasts. (Ezek 23:20–21)

Note how this passage ends with a switch to second-person feminine singular speech. This marks a transition to the next section in which Oholibah is addressed directly by YHWH, as he pronounces her coming judgment. Addressing judgment directly to her is rhetorically more powerful than doing so through a third party. The forthcoming judgment does not differ significantly from what was related in chapter 16, involving stripping, swords, and fire. YHWH declares that the severity of her punishment will accomplish his goal—an end to her whoring and the lust that inspired it (Ezek 23:27). What does differ from chapter 16, however, is the portrayal of the woman as an agent whose gaze objectifies the males on whom it is directed, rather than depicting her as the passive subject of the male gaze (Galambush: 116). Not surprisingly, YHWH reacts by returning the men to a position of power and subjectivity from which they proceed to punish her for her impertinence (Ezek 23:22–24).

At v. 36, YHWH returns to addressing the prophet, commissioning him to declare judgment on the sisters. Here adultery and idolatry are explicitly linked—"with their idols they have committed adultery" (Ezek 23:37)—an unpacking of the metaphor rarely seen. The charge of infanticide is then leveled against the women once again, but with a slight twist. On the same day in which they offer their children as sacrifices to their idols, they enter the temple of YHWH, apparently to worship, but nevertheless desecrating the temple. They come with blood on their hands, the sacrificial blood of their own children, no less—an act that, whether cultic or otherwise, is commonly condemned in the Prophets.

The chapter ends, unlike chapter 16, with unmitigated violence. "[T]he punishment that earlier prophets conceived of as a corrective measure, Ezekiel recasts as the woman's imminent death" (Galambush: 86). Verses 46–49 switch from third-person feminine plural (with some confusion be-

---

40. Hebrew uncertain.

tween feminine plural and masculine plural) address to second-person feminine plural address. The destruction of vv. 24–26 is reiterated, but the ultimate purpose at this point in the chapter is to serve as a warning to all women (Ezek 23:48), a qualification of the punishment that seems oddly trans-metaphoric. This slippage is disturbing in its implications for real flesh-and-blood women, intensified by the fact that it is at this verse in the section that the speech switches to a second-person feminine plural audience, emphasizing the sense that real women as a collective are being addressed.

All in all, Ezekiel surpasses both Hosea and Jeremiah in his usage of the marriage metaphor as a way to strip the woman of any trace of subjectivity. She is rendered as hopelessly perverse and deviant. Hosea's metaphor really was more of a family than marriage metaphor, and the sense was of a dysfunctional family trying to work through a seemingly irreparable breach. This is not to deny that the family was under the strict control of the patriarch/deity, but the family members did not seem completely without voice and personhood. Jeremiah is less interested in family dynamics, illustrated by his omission of a name for the woman, and the mention of children only tangentially; when they are mentioned it is often outside the marriage rhetoric entirely (Jer 3:21–22). Jeremiah's oracles throughout chapters 2 and 3 move back and forth between female and male addressees, creating a disjointed "narrative" that diminishes the impression that a genuine relationship is being worked out. Ezekiel on the other hand sticks quite closely to the metaphor, but creates the impression of an excessively one-sided relationship. The woman (and women) might be given a name, but that is the extent of her subjectivity. She is not provided the merest fissure in which to insert her selfhood. Ezekiel/YHWH tightly controls the discourse from beginning to end. The extreme monologism of the text does violence to the woman as she is silenced through sheer power; and, in this case, content matches form as the prophet is free to inflict extreme verbal abuse, with images of sexual violence graphic enough to be called pornographic.[41] It is good in this context to remember A. Rich's injunction that subjectivity is not only gendered, but is also firmly embodied. Zion's subjectivity is stripped from her, literally, not only in the way that YHWH's discourse constructs and constrains her, but also in the actual violence done to her body.

---

41. Many feminist critics have labeled the texts covered in this chapter, especially those of Jeremiah and Ezekiel, pornographic. A. Brenner discusses pornography as "more than merely an attempt at erotic rather than aesthetic stimulation. It involves social factors such as power, domination, gender relations, and quite often violence . . . and the *function* of pornography is to maintain male dominance through the denial or misnaming of female sexual experience. Objectification of the female is presented as universally acknowledged instead of being attributed to male predisposition against femaleness" (90, 95).

In terms of extracting a dialogic theology from these texts, the possibilities move from bad to worse. Hosea starts his discourse with images
of an actual, albeit troubled, relationship that morphs into a metaphoric
one that still, at least, remains anchored to the relationship between two
actual subjects. Jeremiah, through his use of quotes, as contrived as they
are, allows us a glimpse behind the hegemonic discourse. His style leaves
room to construct a (partial) subjectivity for the woman. Ezekiel closes the
gaps and hence portrays a deity that is interested in little else than absolute domination—of both discourse and persons. Thus, read successively,
these texts evince a growing anxiety.

> The idea that the main/male voice cannot tolerate a rival self and seeks
> to subjugate and eradicate it suggests that every sign of female power-
> lessness in this text, and every offence to the feminist reader can be read
> deconstructively as evidence of women's power. From this perspective,
> the text is *suspiciously* anxious to censor the woman's voice and to create
> a passive woman who plays the part that is given her, speaks the words
> that are prescribed for her. . . .[42] (Sherwood 1996:306)

Although Ezekiel, more than the others, references the covenant to speak
of the link between God and the woman, the term emanates little to no
warmth or reciprocity. Allowing for their differences, all the prophets
assume that Zion is to blame for her loss of subjectivity, that she has abandoned her *true* identity and selfhood through her rebellion. It is suggested,
paradoxically, that she must achieve real subjectivity in servitude. All said,
the formation of a satisfying dialogic theology grounded in the marriage
metaphor must await the woman's own speech, which finally resounds in
the protest discourse of Lam 1–2.

---

42. YHWH's insecurity is represented in other ways, too. Y. Sherwood, chapter 3, shows how the marriage metaphor deconstructs its own rhetoric in several
other ways, as well: YHWH is portrayed as ethically and chronologically superior
to Baal and yet "far from emphasizing YHWH's autonomy and individuality, the
text remakes him in the image of Baal. Baal is perceived by the woman as lover
and provider, and to reclaim her affections, YHWH describes himself in precisely
the same terms" (224).

# 3

## Beyond Form Criticism
### READING GENRE DIALOGICALLY

*To speak in the desired way is . . . to also learn how to speak against oneself.* (Leela Gandhi, *Postcolonial Theory*)

In this chapter I demonstrate the ways in which Lam 1–2 fashions a response to the prophets in terms of linguistic and formal structures, specifically in its reworking of the lament psalms genre. Martin Buss has called for a more relational approach to our form-critical endeavors. In his attendance to the connection between form and life, H. Gunkel's work presaged this call, but in the end his categories were too narrow:

> In observing connections between aspects of literary form, biblical scholarship can go further than Gunkel did, for he reflected on their nature only intermittently. One can ask on a more regular basis, "How does this language go with certain thoughts and feelings, and how do these go with a given kind of situation?" (Buss: 415)

Bakhtin's insistence on the dialogic nature of language and life, from units of language as fundamental as the word to the most complex of utterances can contribute to the goal Buss outlines. Both Gunkel and Bakhtin were interested in speech/texts in their contexts, but Gunkel stressed the fixity of genres, while Bakhtin stressed their fluidity. For Gunkel, genres became impure when altered;[1] for Bakhtin, that is what genres do—change—depending on situation of the "user" (Buss: 259).[2] The intermixing and evolution of genres is a form of artistic expression, not corruption. Com-

---

1. According to Buss, Gunkel held to an Aristotelian essentialism in believing that genres have a distinct "pure" form. Many others during Gunkel's day held to a more flexible view of genres (Buss: 255–56).

2. That is, either the speaker/author or addressee/reader. According to Bakhtin, "Speech genres in general submit fairly easily to reaccentuation; the sad can be made jocular and gay, but as a result something new is achieved" (1986:87). But Bakhtin did acknowledge that the high and official genres are "compulsory and extremely stable" (1986:79).

munication is enabled because of the way in which we manipulate the features of our generic inheritances (Van Leeuwen: 74–75). To ensure form criticism's viability as a hermeneutical tool, we must move beyond an understanding of forms as static constructs and begin to read form dynamically—as content given shape by a living, situated human being—and to recognize that the text has relationships and is responsive to related texts and forms.[3] C. Newsom makes this observation a cornerstone of her understanding of genre and approach to reading biblical forms:

> [T]exts do not "belong" to genres so much as participate in them, invoke them, gesture to them, play in and out of them, and in so doing continually change them. Texts may participate in more than one genre, just as they may be marked in an exaggerated or in a deliberately subtle fashion. The point is not simply to identify a genre in which a text participates, *but to analyze that participation in terms of the rhetorical strategies of the text.*[4] (12, emphasis mine)

In their comprehensive overview of the current state of form criticism, M. Sweeney and E. Ben Zvi also recognize that the method's future lies with this insight:

> Form-critical studies will no longer concern themselves only or mainly with the typical features of language and text. Rhetorical criticism and communication theory have amply demonstrated that the communicative and persuasive functions of texts depend on the unique as well as the typical. Moreover, in considering the rhetorical or communicative aspects of texts, form-critical scholars will no longer presume that genres are static or ideal entities that never change. Rather, they will recognize the inherent fluidity of genres, the fact that they are historically, culturally, and discursively dependent, *and they will study the means by which genres are transformed to meet the needs of the particular communicative situation of the text.* (9–10, emphasis mine)

Accordingly, a proper definition of genre must stress flexibility as much as stability: "[T]he fact that a genre can retain its identity in the face of sometimes radical changes in its linguistic and cultural environment illustrates the flexibility of the genre's rule and its ability to absorb 'culture shock' " (Fishelov: 8, 17). In this chapter, I read Lam 1–2 as a product of the "culture shock" of 587 B.C.E.,[5] and in so doing explore the ways in which it remains identifiable as a member of the lament genre, as well as the way it is transformed "to meet the needs of the particular communicative situation of the

---

3. As such, my architectonics of reading involves orchestrating parts into wholes that are nevertheless dynamic and transitional because I accept Bakhtin's emphasis on texts as "radically perspectival and situational" (Holquist: xxviii).

4. In this description, Newsom also implies the difficulty in generically labeling a given text, an issue I address below.

5. See D. Smith-Christopher (2002: ch. 2) for an appreciation of the devastation suffered by the Judeans at the hands of the Babylonians.

text."[6] P. Tull says addressing the poles of continuity and change requires a balancing act between the methods of form and rhetorical criticism:

> [The] tension between the typical and the unique has come to represent somewhat of a fault line between form critics and rhetorical critics. Insofar as form critics sort texts into generic categories, they lay hold of a very real aspect of texts, that is, their defining relationship to other texts. But insofar as they submerge a text's uniqueness, they risk ignoring where a text stands *in relation to* the genres it inhabits. Rhetorical criticism takes equal and opposite risks. Insofar as rhetorical critics focus on a unique text, analyzing its own internal logic and rhetorical patterning, they risk ignoring the role of other texts both in this text's shaping by authors and in its comprehension by readers. (327)

In my reading, however, the ultimate rhetorical purpose for reworking the features of traditional generic lament is to craft a response to the prophetic rhetoric that exploited the marriage metaphor as a staging ground for its accusations against Israel.

An anecdotal analogy may prove a useful starting point: I spent July 2004 in Manhattan involved in a research colloquium,[7] where I had the opportunity to attend a Broadway musical that illustrates the way genres morph so as to continue to convey meaningfully in new contexts. *Wicked* is a retelling of a modern musical cinematic fairy tale, *The Wizard of Oz*.[8] It was perfectly recognizable structurally and semiotically as drawing on the conventions of that genre—music, good versus evil, talking animals, didactic motifs, overcoming fearsome situations and opponents, and so on—but it reshuffled its signifiers to suit its postmodern/postcolonial intentions. The story is retold from the perspective of the wicked witch, who is merely trying to defend the subjugated (subaltern), indigenous creatures in her kingdom from the oppressive imperial policies of the Wizard (an "outsider"), which include the removal of their ability to speak, literally. The witch, who in this version is given a name, "Elphaba," a twist that

---

6. All said, the extent to which the morphological elements of Lam 1–2 and lament psalms tally is very much subordinated to other factors, such as emotional and physical context, mood, psychological and social function, and so on (on this point, see B. Green [2003:xv–xvi]). Similar generic and theological reshuffling has been noted during the period of Ugaritic social and political upheaval that led to the eventual downfall of the city-state (see de Moor).

7. I am very grateful to CrossCurrents for their support of this chapter while I was their guest as a Coolidge Fellow at Union Theological Seminary in New York, summer 2004.

8. I am comparing *Wicked*—the theatrical version, as opposed to the book by G. Maguire—to the 1939 screen version of the movie, *The Wizard of Oz*, rather than to the original book (*The Wonderful Wizard of Oz*) by L. F. Baum because of the film's iconic status and the fact that the creators of *Wicked*, the musical, were working from a similar assumption.

is crucial to underlining her subjectivity, is given the opportunity to tell her side of the story and is thus able to construct a persona that defies the construction previously applied to her by the Wizard and by the story/ genre itself. The unmasking of the perceived redeemer as an oppressor is a message that is readily comprehensible, even embraced, among large segments of contemporary North American society. And in fact, the play has been wildly popular, selling out for months and months and garnering a remarkable ten Tony Award nominations. This is largely because a postmodern reworking of the mythic conventions of fairytales (good vs. evil, the hero's journey, etc.) resonates with some Americans at this time in a way that the original no longer does. A remake that strove to remain rigidly loyal to the original would seem quaint rather than compelling.

As crucial to the definition of genre as is the notion of flexibility, of course, is the more common and integral observation that genres also exert a restrictive influence, albeit a pliable restriction, on our expression. Ironically, this constraint is necessary for individual creativity. *Wicked* would not have been nearly so effective from a creative standpoint had it disregarded completely the features of the original form. In fact, much of the play's power derives from its recognizability: Elphaba is still green, still dressed in black, and still unleashes that cackle when vanquishing her enemies. She is completely identifiable on an iconic level, but no one who sees *Wicked* can ever "read" her character the same way again. Likewise, a committed reading of Lam 1–2 compels a reappraisal of Daughter Zion as she is construed in a number of prophetic texts. As I suggest, the poet of Lamentations draws part of his rhetorical impact from the maintenance of the female metaphor for Israel. In this way, the poet provides his audience with a recognizable voice for their pain. Repeating the shameful figuration of Israel as female might seem an odd choice if the goal is *comfort*, but in light of the treatment this figure receives at the hand of YHWH in the prophetic texts, granting this voice subjectivity makes a powerful and corrective theological statement.

## The Setup

Israel had at least one indigenous genre (or two related genres), besides the dirge, that could be deployed in situations of individual and corporate anxiety—individual (and communal) psalms of lament, or complaint.[9] And

_____

9. As I have noted elsewhere, I prefer the designation "grievance psalms" because it better captures the active, almost performative nature of this speech (Mandolfo: 1). As far as the division of the genre into "individual" and "communal," it seems rather arbitrary. The old argument over whether "I-psalms" were in reality corporate exposes the difficulty in delineating between the two. Issues of setting are clearly at stake in the effort to delineate, but in a more purely literary context, it seems to matter less. And in fact, it is arguable that the poems in the Book of Lamentations are as much individual as they are communal. In chapters 1

surely many of them, like Lamentations, were composed or preserved, at least, in response to 587 B.C.E. A look at the first two chapters of Lamentations, however, suggests that some members of the community needed an outlet for their grief that, while still drawing on established generic traditions, was tailored to this particular situation.[10] This chapter focuses on some of the particulars of how the poet went about his task, but this goal ultimately answers more far-reaching questions: why did the poet make the choices he did; and what ideological goals did he hope to accomplish? Trying to unravel ideological motivations necessarily involves attending to generic usage: "The choice of genre over and against other conventional literary discourses is already an ideological act. Motivations might be recovered by asking questions such as: *How does the text conform to the conventions of the genre, and how does it depart from them? It is in these departures that the text reworks the ideology that intrudes between it and history"* (Yee 2003:26, emphasis mine).

I focus on the two chapters of Lamentations in which the people are figured as a woman—*bat Zion*—because they hold together as a unit through the use of the feminine metaphor. Furthermore, the metaphor gives me a point of entry for discussing in the most tangible ways possible my proposition that these two chapters function as a "response" to both the devastation of 587 B.C.E. and the way in which the devastation was prefigured in the marriage-metaphor rhetoric of the prophetic texts.[11] In short, I understand the rhetorical (if not socio-psychological) *impetus* of Lam 1–2 as providing Daughter Zion a voice to speak back to the accusations leveled against her in the Prophets, and I see the reworking of the lament-psalm genre as the *means* of reaching that goal.

I chart the "development" from lament to Lamentations primarily by attending to formal features, specifically the way voices are aligned in the various texts. As I have demonstrated elsewhere, many individual laments are, in spite of a history of monologic interpretation, actually double-voiced

---

and 2, *bat Zion* is the main supplicant, even if she is speaking for the collective. To avoid dealing with a distinction that does not matter for this study, I refer to both individual and communal as merely "lament."

10. As Van Leeuwen notes, "[L]iterary production permits the adaptation of primary genres to new contexts, functions, and the creation of new genres, or of previous literary genres. This generic fecundity is rampant in Scripture" (81).

11. Generic responsivity is integral to Bakhtin's dialogic linguistics: "Every utterance must be regarded primarily as a *response* to preceding utterances of the given sphere (we understand the word 'response' here in the broadest sense). Each utterance refutes, affirms, supplements, and relies on the others, presupposes them to be known, and somehow takes them into account.... *It is impossible to determine its position without correlating it with other positions*" (1986:91). Interestingly, Buss notes that the Jewish thinker, Israel Abrahams, in his 1920 study *Poetry and Religion* understood the psalms as a "response" to God's speaking through the prophets (375).

(Mandolfo 2002). I flesh this out more thoroughly shortly, but it suffices for now to say that the supplicant's voice is combined in these psalms with what I have called a "Didactic Voice" (hereafter "DV"), a third-person voice that speaks *of* and *for* rather than *to* God, and is thus a didactic, rather than prayerful, discourse. The interplay of the DV and the supplicant results in an ideologically tensive discourse that remains open-ended and unresolved throughout the Psalter. Lamentations 1–2, even more explicitly than the psalms, features two voices—the supplicant (Daughter Zion) and an objective or third-person voice—but in this case the third-person voice is co-opted into the ideological world of the supplicant's discourse, with the result that the tension that prevails in the lament psalms seems somewhat relieved in Lamentations. This rhetorical relief, however, comes at the cost of stable or comforting theology. Whereas the DV in the psalms of lament could be construed as speaking in support of the prophetic utterances regarding divine retributive justice, that same voice in Lam 1–2 has structurally reversed its former perspective and now stands with the supplicant, more or less against the deity and the prophets through whom the deity speaks. Lamentations 1–2 is the only dialogic text in the Bible, of which I am aware, in which this alignment takes place. Even in Job, an intensely dialogic and confrontational text, the countervoices—manifested in the persons of the friends—uphold a "prophetic" point of view: "Does God pervert justice?" (Job 8:3).

I have carefully laid out my dialogic reading of psalms elsewhere, but I will outline it here for the sake of my thesis regarding Lamentations. In many psalms of lament, particularly those usually referred to as "individual," a didactic voice that speaks of God in third-person descriptive terms is interjected into the supplicant's second-person discourse directed toward God—it speaks to the supplicant in the form of a command. This latter voice could be understood as revelatory insofar as it speaks as a mouthpiece for, or in defense of, the deity. Biblical speech includes both receptive/revelatory (prophets and priestly) and active speech (prayers and wisdom), but these two come together in psalms of lament (Buss: 26, 29). This configuration is fairly clear in Ps 7 (the underlined sections belong to the DV):[12]

v. 1  A Shiggayon of David which he sang to YHWH concerning the deeds of Cush, the Benjaminite.
v. 2  YHWH, my god, in you I trust.
      Save me from all who pursue me, and rescue me,
v. 3  lest he rend my soul like a lion, tearing [it] apart,
      and there is none to rescue [me].
v. 4  YHWH, my god, if I have done this,
      if there is iniquity in my palms;

---

12. Much of the following analysis of Ps 7 is drawn from my previous work, *God in the Dock*.

v. 5   If I have repaid evil to one at peace with me
       (instead, though, I have delivered, in vain, the one vexing
       me),
v. 6   let the enemy persecute my soul, and entrap,
       and trample my life to the earth; and lay my honor in the
       dust.

v. 7   Arise, YHWH, in your anger;
       lift yourself up against the fury of those vexing me.
       Rouse yourself on my behalf.
       Ordain fairness!
v. 8   Let the congregation of the tribes encompass you,
       and for their sake return to the high place [seat of
       judgment?].

v. 9   YHWH arbitrates between the peoples;

       judge me, YHWH, according to my innocence,
       and according to my integrity within me.
v. 10  Let the wickedness of the evil ones cease,
       and establish the just.

       The one who tests the thoughts and emotions is a just god.

v. 11  My defense depends on a god
       who saves the upright of heart.

v. 12  God is a just judge, but a god who is indignant every day.
v. 13  If one does not turn back then He whets his sword,
       He has bent his bow and readied it.
v. 14  And He has readied for himself instruments of death—
       He has made arrows into burning ones.

v. 15  Observe! He pledges iniquity, and conceives trouble,
       and gives birth to falsehood.
v. 16  He has dug a ditch and hollowed it out,
       and fallen into the pit he made.
v. 17  His trouble will return on his own head
       and upon his scalp his violence will descend.

v. 18  I will praise YHWH according to his justice,
       and I will sing the name of YHWH Elyon.

The psalm begins and ends with the supplicant's discourse, as do many of
the multivoiced prayers in the Psalter. The early part of the psalm, consisting mostly of petition and a setting forth of the case, can be ascribed to
the petitioner, while the latter part of the psalm (except for the last verse)
seems to belong to another voice that provides a wisdom-like lesson on the
fate of evildoers. The middle portion of the psalm alternates between the

petitioner's and another's voice. Furthermore, the two voices seem to be responding to one another fairly directly. The short instructional discourse in v. 9a is centrally located in the psalm and should, perhaps, along with the petition of v. 9b, be understood as embodying the main themes (judgment and justice) of both of the discourses. A closer look at grammatical details will help explicate this structure.

The supplicant's voice can be identified by the use of first-person common singular verbs and pronouns throughout the early portion of the psalm. This voice directly addresses the deity, using second-person masculine singular pronouns in the address. Highlighting the urgency of the supplicant's petition, masculine singular imperatives are employed by the supplicant in vv. 2, 7, and 8. The shift from second-person masculine singular direct address to third-person masculine singular in v. 9 signals a new voice. A segue is provided by v. 8 in which there is no use of first-person common singular speech to indicate that the supplicant is still speaking. Still, the ongoing use of masculine singular imperatives makes it fairly clear that v. 8 is a continuation of v. 7.[13] The didactic interjection in v. 9a makes a general claim about YHWH's attributes, using third-person masculine singular speech. Immediately following, moving back to the more particular case of the supplicant, YHWH is addressed again, directly, by the supplicant, who renews her plea for personal salvation. The plea in v. 9b can be understood as responding directly to the previous interjection, using similar, but not identical terminology: Verse 9a uses דין while v. 9b uses מפט, the first being in the indicative to describe a quality, the second being in the imperative to make a request. In other words, the supplicant responds to a description of one of YHWH's attributes by requesting that YHWH act in a way consistent with that attribute. Verse 10a moves back to the theme of universal judgment (recompensing the wicked and just according to their deserts), but continues the style of the supplicant, using imperatives to direct YHWH's actions. Verse 10b may shift again; the deity is once again described, not addressed. With this interjection, the supplicant is offered assurance that God is capable of answering her request.

Verse 12 serves as an introduction to a final, lengthy instructional section that extends through v. 17. Verse 12 is set off from the concluding didactic section in that, as with the previous didactic sections, it speaks of divine attributes, while vv. 13–17 describe the fate of the wicked. As we have seen with other verses in this psalm, vv. 11 and 12 can be read as dialogue. In other words, reading for content only, it makes sense to read v. 12 as a response to v. 11—Supplicant: "My defense depends on a god who saves the upright of heart." Respondent: "God *is* a just judge, but a god who is indignant everyday." As with much of the psalm, reading dialogically helps make sense of the repetition that occurs in these two verses. Rhetorically,

---

13. Verse 8 is notoriously difficult to translate, making it nearly impossible to argue to which discourse it belongs.

this interpretation makes sense as well. It seems reasonable to read v. 12 as an introductory statement to vv. 13–17 (as well as a response to v. 11).

v. 11 My defense depends on a god who saves the upright of heart.

v. 12 God is a just judge, but a god who is indignant every day.

v. 13 If one does not turn back then He whets his sword, He has bent his bow and readied it.

v. 14 And He has readied for himself instruments of death— He has made arrows into burning ones.

v. 15 Observe! He pledges iniquity, and conceives trouble, and gives birth to falsehood.

v. 16 He has dug a ditch and hollowed it out, and fallen into the pit he made.

v. 17 His trouble will return on his own head and upon his scalp his violence will descend.

In v. 12, God is described as a judge with the emphasis on his harsh judgments. The following verses then go on to describe how God's judgment is played out against the iniquitous. More precisely, v. 12a echoes v. 11, while v. 12b announces the theme taken up in vv. 13–17. Even if we accept that v. 12 does belong to a voice other than the supplicant and is connected to the following verses, it still must be shown that vv. 13–17 do not fit the rhetoric of the supplicant.

It seems somewhat illogical to assign vv. 13–17 to the supplicant (although scholars often do it). It seems unlikely that the voice that petitions the deity in a time of crisis to intercede against her enemies is the same voice that confidently asserts a universal order that assures the self-destruction of the wicked. Trying to make sense of these verses as part of the discourse of the petitioner, E. Gerstenberger understands vv. 13–15 as the resumption of the supplicant's complaint (v. 3) and vv. 16–17 as an imprecation against, or condemnation of, the enemies (63–65). He seems perplexed by his own explanation: "Strangely enough, there is another round of complaining and of condemning enemies" (65). He explains this in light of "the ceremonial procedure": "The supplication has to be repetitive in order to reach the divine addressee" (65). Although possible, this explanation seems to complicate the data. These verses are not suggestive in form or content of either complaint or imprecation. Even Gerstenberger recognizes that vv. 16–17 "are proverbial in character," but insists that they "are here used in imprecative form" (65). In fact, "proverbial" is a term that could be used to describe all of vv. 13–17. As Gerstenberger clearly recognizes, they have a didactic bent and do not fit the previous rhetorical style used by the supplicant in the early part of the psalm.[14] In short, the

---

14. A. Weiser also notes the didactic quality of these verses (139).

psalm begins with a petition but ends (penultimately) with a moral lesson, not with further complaints by the supplicant. The instructional discourse acts as a response to the petition.[15] We do not hear a discourse that seems clearly to belong to the supplicant again until the vow of praise in v. 18, the rationale for which can be seen in the instruction imparted in vv. 12–17. After the extended reassurance that YHWH has the just governance of the cosmos well in hand, the supplicant seems satisfied and in the final verse vows praise to YHWH. That the supplicant offers praise only after a detailed accounting of the fate of the wicked makes it clear that vindication for her consists primarily in the destruction of her enemies. At the core of the psalm is the issue of what constitutes divine justice.

To summarize, note how the DV counters the supplicant's shaky faith in God's justice (or at least the deity's current application of it) and insists that God delivers justice according to deserts. The two voices/positions seem to respond to one another until the end, where the supplicant seems satisfied by the insistence on God's fairness. What interests me most is the rhetorical interplay of these voices and the way they offer a dialogic theological point of view—one that implies the manifest unfairness of much of existence—"Ordain fairness!" (v. 7)—and the other that posits the "normative" theology of the Bible that proclaims "God is a just judge!" (v. 12). What makes these dialogical, in the Bakhtinian sense, is not merely the form of dialogue that I suggest for them (dialogue can be monological), but the perception that two worldviews are interacting.[16] Both are altered by the interaction and forced to "tilt" their position, so to speak. The DV's worldview is decentered, its centripetal tendencies resisted, while the supplicant's complaint is clearly constrained by the generic demand, imposed by the cult, no doubt, to avoid blasphemous speech. This tension characterizes nearly all laments, suggesting it is a requisite feature of the genre, a feature Lam 1–2 will both foreground and yet nevertheless subvert.

When close attention is paid to the dialogic form of laments, the decentering force each voice exerts on the other becomes manifest, but the overall control the DV, as the "revelatory" voice, exerts is still hard to overcome. The genre is, after all, a religious or cultic creation and is primarily in the service of upholding God's authority.[17] The lament genre has a specific ideological agenda, and all voices contained within it are compelled,

---

15. The use of אם to start v. 13 is reminiscent of both wisdom literature (particularly Proverbs) and casuistic pentateuchal law. The use of a third-person referent is closer to the style used in biblical law texts than proverbial texts, the latter being typically couched in a second-person dialogue format.

16. It is possible to chart this interplay even in those psalms that are structurally and grammatically single-voiced, but it is simpler to see in those that are double-voiced.

17. In fact, it is the genres of ritual (and lament psalms are surely the verbal portion of what was a more encompassing lament ritual) that create and maintain

more or less effectively, to be at its service. Hence, one rarely hears from scholars a focus on that aspect of the lament psalm that suggests YHWH is unreliable, or unfair. This has much to do with the form itself—the way in which the protests are generally presented grammatically in the first and second person makes the supplicant's speech more personal, subjective, less authoritative. Conversely, the DV's viewpoint is expressed almost exclusively in the third person, lending it an air of objectivity and prestige.[18] As Morson and Emerson report about highly authoritative utterances (of which they cite scripture as an example), "There [is] a tendency to 'depersonalize' and 'disembody' the authoritative figure's speech, so that it is not perceived as merely one person's opinion" (164). In Lam 1–2, on the other hand, the voice of the supplicant does not have to compete with a countervoice. As will be demonstrated, the DV's authoritative third-person structure lends clout to *bat Zion*'s discourse. Regardless, commentators have persisted in privileging a theologically normative voice over the voice of protest; in other words, Zion got what she deserved.[19] The theological orthodoxy of the DV is a generic feature of laments that the poet of Lam 1–2 amends to disquieting effect.

Thus far, I have been assuming that Lam 1–2 is a "type" of lament, but the designation of a genre is an ongoing dispute in Lamentations scholarship. Most agree that Lamentations constitutes a mixed genre—*qinah* (or dirge) and lament.[20] Lamentations 3 and 5 follow fairly purely the typical form of psalmic laments. That *qinot* contain no appeal for deliverance, unlike laments, strengthens their tie to Lam 1–2, which also omits any explicit appeal.[21] No *qinot* have survived in the Bible; all we are left with are literary creations crafted for narrative (e.g., 2 Sam 1:17) and prophetic (e.g., Jer 9:9) purposes. Although Lamentations clearly also has affinities with Mesopotamian city laments, it is impossible to determine the precise connection between the two.[22] Despite the formal similarities (such as the

---

a type of religious and socio-political authority known as "traditional authority," according to M. Bloch (71).

18. There are places in the psalms where YHWH's praises are sung in a first- and second-person voice, but grievance is strictly limited to first and second person.

19. This bias has been corrected in recent commentaries/monographs by T. Linafelt, K. O'Connor, A. Berlin, F. W. Dobbs-Allsopp.

20. Rabbinic literature designates Lamentations (as well as Pss 3 and 79) a *qinah* (Berlin: 23). F. W. Dobbs-Allsopp lists the elements of the dirge genre in Lam 1: opening particle (*'eykah*); contrast motif; Jerusalem as a widow; and the *qinah* meter (2002:54).

21. D. Hillers calls Lam 1, 2, and 4 dirges, for the most part, but sees them as very mixed genres (xxvii).

22. Dobbs-Allsopp considers the city lament the most "important" generic influence on Lamentations (2002:9–11). See A. Berlin for a skeptical assessment of Mesopotamian influence (27). Patricia Tull Willey notes that Mesopotamian

feminization of the city, which, obviously, is of no small consequence to this study), there are some significant differences. The Mesopotamian city laments seem to have as their primary function the rebuilding of the city and the return of the gods to the city. This comic trajectory has more of an affinity with Second Isaiah than Lamentations, which takes a tragic tack (Dobbs-Allsopp 2002:11). And theologically, they could not be more dissimilar. The city laments portray gods that have acted capriciously in their destruction of the city,[23] while in Lamentations, of course, it is implied that YHWH is inflicting punishment with good reason (although I will problematize this notion later in the chapter).

Whatever the influence of the city laments, Adele Berlin claims that the combination of *qinah* and lament in Lamentations (and in Pss 44, 69, 74, 79, 102, and 137) results in a new genre, which she calls the "Jerusalem lament" (24–25). Berlin is sensitive to the complexity that attends the changes that genres undergo and says that the Jerusalem lament is more than the mere combination of *qinah* and lament.[24] She also recognizes the generative role social context is bound to play: "This new genre or subgenre arose from a new historical situation and a new theological need" (25). Lamentations as a whole may have some similarities to the psalms she has labeled as Jerusalem laments, but these similarities are mainly thematic, arising from a shared historical situation. And taken independently, Lam 1–2 certainly does not have enough in common with Berlin's new genre to share a designation. While not feeling obliged to support her opinion that a new genre emerged out of 587 B.C.E., I do agree with her basic thesis—that 587 was enough of a rupture to the socio-psychological fabric of ancient Israel that it provoked the emergence of a fresh, if not sustained, version of lam-

---

lament literature highlights the motif of the " 'weeping goddess,' the protector of the people who mourns her destroyed city and intercedes in the divine assembly. . . . In Mesopotamian literature, in which the word 'city' is masculine or neuter, the goddess functioned as a patron, mother of the unpersonified city. In West Semitic languages 'city' was feminine, and the city itself was understood as a goddess, married to the patron god of the city" (279). This inability to divinize the feminized city allows for more compelling theological connections because we are allowed to look closely at a relationship between God and a human rather than two deities.

23. "The Curse of Agade" is an exception. The ruler Naram Sin is guilty and responsible for the destruction of his kingdom (Dobbs-Allsopp 2002:9). Still, that is a very different thrust than the assertion that the people as a whole are responsible. Because of a lack of a direct relationship between the gods and the people as a whole, Mesopotamian literature lacks the emphasis on the doctrine of retribution that is so prevalent in the Bible (Jerrold Cooper in private conversation, New York, July 2004).

24. She suggests that "Zion songs" may also have exerted an influence. Songs that originally sung the praises of the city after 587 B.C.E. were no longer appropriate, and the city's shame was put to song instead (Berlin: 25).

entation; and that the generic ingredients that went into this new form of expression are multiple, so that the influence they exert is too complex to chart with precision.

Since we do not have a solid example of a *qinah* in ancient Israel, this study will not take up the task of trying to explain how Lam 1–2 evolved from that direction; and Dobbs-Allsopp has already done a thorough evaluation of the relationship between Lamentations and the city laments (1993). By suggesting that Lam 1–2 represents a development of the lament tradition, I am not trying to make a positivistic claim about genre, that Lam 1–2 is somehow more closely related to lament psalms than to dirges, or to city laments. I do feel justified in making the claim, however, that there are clearer "family resemblances" between the two.[25] If nothing else, Lamentations is a "form" of lament, sharing such elements as subject, values, mood, style (to some degree), task (to some degree), attitude, and occasion (i.e., threat).[26] With regard to the biblical corpus as a whole, they are among the few texts that speak in large part *to* YHWH rather than *about* YHWH. The poet of Lamentations surely borrowed freely from the generic traditions that surrounded him without engaging in much theoretical reflection, but because we have inherited a well-established lament tradition in the Bible, from a readerly perspective, at least, it is natural for us to read Lamentations as a lament (and lexical connections between Lamentations and Psalms have long been noted) (Hillers: xxii).

## The Reading

My focus on the links between Lam 1–2 and psalmic laments will involve both content and formal features. As mentioned, Lam 1–2, far more explicitly than psalms of lament, is a double- (or multi-) voiced utterance.

---

25. See A. Fowler for a discussion of texts within a genre as representing types that share traits, rather than as fixed entities. It is useful to keep in mind the qualification of A. Berlin: We cannot know whether Lamentations is more *qinah* than lament or vice versa, nor do we have to choose to produce a "good" reading (24). B. Green makes a related observation about the relative arbitrariness of genre choice: "If the author does not, or has not in this instance, been able to signal the genre clearly, and if those wishing to gather the genre's identity from a scrutiny of its literary DNA fail, is it simply a reader's call? . . . [M]y genre needs to be generally coherent with what that author would have been supposing, unless, of course, I am consciously choosing to read counter to the 'culturally viable product' that we have. . . . The genre definition I offer will need to include fairly well the literary features of the book. It will not be exact, of course, since art is not following formulas rigidly. But my definition needs to work with most of the elements in the narrative. It will be shown effective . . . as I do the work of showing the way in which 'my genre choice' produces an effective, compelling reading of the story" (2005: 91).

26. These are some of the generic categories established in A. Fowler (61).

The speech of "characters" is clearly delineated, and voices/discourses alternate in ways quite like some of the psalms. In Bakhtinian terms, Lamentations *as a whole* comes closer to genuine polyphony than most biblical texts (although in Lam 1–2, Daughter Zion's voice dominates for reasons this chapter will point out). Voices are woven together with no perspective dominating the others, not even the narrator's (Heim: 169). Points of view are nuanced, and allusions to former texts and traditions abound. For my comparison with Lam 1–2, I concentrate on only two double-voiced laments—Ps 22 and Lam 3—although I touch on others to make certain points. Psalm 22 provides a fairly clear contrast to the rhetoric of Daughter Zion in Lamentations, and Lam 3 is a classic lament that because of contiguity serves as a good counterpoint to the poems that precede it. Because of the inherent difficulties in establishing actual development, at one level, it could be argued that I am doing little more than reading intertextually. But an intertextual reading of the two genres is a productive undertaking in its own right, as it can result in fresh theological observations, not to mention a better understanding of the formal and rhetorical features of the text. Furthermore, intertextual work is of course an integral part of form-critical work. Bakhtin recognized that dialogic forces are at work when any two utterances are juxtaposed on a semantic plane, a phenomenon he called "unintentional dialogicity" (1986:117).

Lamentations 1 begins with a cry—'*eykah*—more appropriate to a dirge than a lament. Unlike many lament psalms, the supplicant's speech does not open the poem, but like laments the focus is on the suffering of the supplicant. Lamentations 1 continues with third-person speech concerning the tribulations of Zion for several verses, so we do not hear Zion herself speak until v. 9. In contrast, but in accord with most lament psalms, Ps 22 begins with the speech of the supplicant and a traditional statement of lamentation: "My God, my God, why have you abandoned me? Why are you so far from saving me, from the words of my complaint?" "Why" is frequently used in lament psalms as a form of complaint against divine inattentiveness: "God, why have you cast us off forever? Why does your anger smoke against the sheep of your pasture?" (74:1); "Why do you hide your face, and forget our affliction and our oppression?" (44:25). Even in the absence of the interrogative, several psalmic supplicants suggest God's culpability in their suffering. Psalm 38, for example, opens up with a plea that emphasizes many of the same concerns that haunt Daughter Zion's rhetoric: God's wrath and his *direct* involvement in the suffering of the supplicant.

> YHWH, rebuke me not in your anger
> nor chasten me in your wrath!
> For your arrows have sunk into me,
> and your hand has come down on me. (38:2–3)

Similar statements are peppered throughout the more impassioned laments: "You have laid me in the lowest pit, in darkness, in the deeps. Your wrath lies hard upon me, and you overwhelm me with all your waves" (88:7–8). A request that naturally arises in the context of such complaint is, however, absent in *bat Zion*'s discourse. Although Daughter Zion frequently demands that her situation be noticed, both by YHWH and passersby, interestingly, she never explicitly requests succor from God. [27] Psalm 22:20–22 is typical of what we are usually treated to:

> But you, O Lord, be not far off;
> my strength, hasten to my aid.
> Save my life from the sword,
> my precious life from the clutches of a dog.
> Deliver me from a lion's mouth;
> from the horns of wild oxen rescue me.

Not only does Daughter Zion neglect to ask YHWH for assistance, but she also, tellingly, fails to address YHWH by any of the appellations in Ps 22 that refer to his saving abilities, such as "my god" and "my strength." In fact, none of the typical metaphors—"rock," "fortress," "just judge," "king," "benefactor"—connected to YHWH in lament psalms is used in Lam 1–2.[28] The one occasion on which she requests that God intervene on her behalf—to exact vengeance on her enemies—betrays little hope that God will directly improve her situation (1:21–22). Even when the DV/narrator in Lam 2 beseeches her to cry out to God as her only hope (2:18–19), she only pours out her rage, but never asks for mercy (2:20–22).

Like many double-voiced psalms (see Ps 7 analysis), after the initial complaint in Ps 22, there is a counterdiscourse that begins at v. 4. The voice does not shift grammatically, but it serves the same rhetorical function as the DV in lament psalms, that is, to balance out the theologically destabilizing complaint that preceded it: God is "holy" and to be "trusted." Lamentations 1–2 includes no such proclamation of confidence. Psalm 22 then rapidly shifts back to complaint—"But I am a worm, and no man; a reproach of men" (v. 7)—and echoes *bat Zion*'s self description in Lamentations: "Look YHWH, and see how worthless I have become!" (Lam 1:11). Psalm 22:12 laments that "there is none to help," similar to *bat Zion*'s cry that she has "no one to comfort" her (1:21). In both, this proclamation is coupled with the observation that enemies are the cause of the problems. Both also suggest that God is behind the enemies' success, although in Ps 22 this suggestion is subtle (mentioned only once in v. 16), while in Lamentations it is declared overtly, over and over again by Zion herself (1:12, 13, 14, 15; 2:20–22), not to mention the numerous times the assessment is affirmed by the narrator/poet in both chapters (but especially in chap-

---

27. Incidentally, this may suggest a significant argument against categorizing Lamentations along with Berlin's other Jerusalem laments.

28. As Dobbs-Allsopp points out, the only metaphor used to describe God is some version of "warrior" (2002:30).

ter 2). From v. 23 until the end of Ps 22 the discourse of the DV takes over (except for a brief reversion to second-person speech in v. 26a). The voicing switches to speech about, rather than to, the deity, and it follows the standard line we find in the didactic discourse of so many laments. Of special interest for a comparison with Lam 1–2 is v. 25: "For he has not despised nor abhorred the affliction of the afflicted; nor has he hid his face from him; but when he cried to him, he heard." Most laments end with similar thanksgiving, but praise of any sort is foreign and, moreover, antithetical to the third-person/narratorial discourse featured in Lam 1–2. In the midst of Zion's grievance in Lam 1 is inserted, instead, third-person speech that reports a purely negative assessment of Zion's situation vis-à-vis God.

> Zion stretches out her hands,
> but there is no one to comfort her;
> YHWH has commanded against Jacob
> that his neighbors should become his foes;
> Jerusalem has become a filthy thing among them. (Lam 1:17)

Even so, in Lam 1 the DV's assessment of Zion's situation still acknowledges some responsibility on her part for what has befallen her (1:5, 8), thus vindicating God to a degree, but in chapter 2, the DV moves much farther from the normative theological position of the psalmic DVs (O'Connor 2002:33–34). Amassed, the verbs used, along with their qualifiers, are uniquely fierce.

> How YHWH in his anger
> has humiliated daughter Zion!
> He has thrown down from heaven to earth
> the splendor of Israel;
> he has not remembered his footstool
> in the day of his anger.
>
> YHWH has destroyed without mercy
> all the dwellings of Jacob;
> in his wrath he has broken down
> the strongholds of daughter Judah;
> he has brought down to the ground
> in dishonor the kingdom and its rulers. (Lam 2:1–2)

B. Kaiser notes that in Lam 2:1–8b there is a "remarkably sustained succession of parallel clauses" that include twenty-nine masculine singular active verbs, "most connoting destruction and all having Yahweh/Adonai as the subject" (177). In accord with this harsh appraisal of YHWH's activities and presaging Zion's own rhetoric in 2:22, the DV in Lam 2:4–5 refers to YHWH as an "enemy." The poet (or later editor) tempers that assessment somewhat by inserting כִּי, thus making YHWH "like" an enemy, a qualification Zion herself does not bother with when she refers to YHWH as "my enemy" at the end of chapter 2.[29]

---

29. Dobbs-Allsopp suggests that the particle is a later addition (2002:83). Xuan Huong Thi Pham says that כִּי means "exactly like" (98).

In contrast to this dismal portrayal of YHWH, Ps 22 ends with the DV assuring the supplicant that future generations shall have reason to praise YHWH's justice:

> Their progeny will serve him;
> it will be told of YHWH to the coming generation.
> They will come,
> and will declare his justice to a people not yet born,
> that he has done this. (22:30–31)

Moreover, the "poor shall eat and be satisfied!" (22:29). Abandoning for a moment the usual third-person address, the DV of Lam 2 (although it is plausible the address belongs to Zion herself) comments on the issues of food and progeny, as well, but from an opposing perspective:

> My eyes are spent with weeping;
> my stomach churns;
> my bile is poured out on the ground
> because of the destruction of my people,
> because infants and babes faint
> in the streets of the city.
>
> They cry to their mothers,
> "Where is bread and wine?"
> as they faint like the wounded
> in the streets of the city,
> as their life is poured out
> on their mothers' bosom. (2:11–12)

Not only is YHWH not providing food, but is withholding it, ensuring that no "progeny will serve him." This hasty comparison of Ps 22 and Lam 1–2 is not meant to suggest that the poet of Lamentations had Ps 22 in mind when reworking the genre, but only to suggest that the situation of 587 B.C.E. compelled some reassessment of how to communicate with God within the tradition of Israelite lament, utilizing well-rehearsed themes and structure. This exercise could be repeated with many lament psalms, but it will suffice to conclude by looking at what amounts to a lament psalm transposed to the Book of Lamentations (Dobbs-Allsopp 2002:105).

Lamentations 3 features a male supplicant, whose discourse opens the poem. In conformity with most laments, the supplicant in Lam 3 is primarily focused on his own suffering and grief, rather than, for example, Lam 1–2's focus on the children. The poem is basically divided into three fairly even sections. Verses 1–21 consist of speech to the deity from the supplicant; vv. 22–42 are spoken by the DV (except for vv. 40–42, which includes mixed voicing); and vv. 43–66, which switches back to the supplicant speaking to the deity, the first part of which reprises the complaint of the first section, the second part of which professes faith in YHWH. Such tight organization suggests a nearly stylized lament, perhaps explainable by the lateness of the poem as well as the liturgical needs demanded by the calamity to which it is responding.[30] Much of the supplicant's discourse about God in chapter 3 matches in intensity and pathos that of Daughter Zion's in the two previous chapters.

> He is to me like a bear lying in wait,
> like a lion in hiding;
> he led me off my way and tore me to pieces;
> he has made me desolate;
> he bent his bow and set me
> as a mark for his arrow. (Lam 3:10–12)

It is in the objective discourse of the DV/narrator where the differences become apparent.[31] In v. 22, following hot on the heels of quite impassioned complaint rhetoric, the tone completely shifts, and the DV proclaims: "The steadfast love of YHWH never ceases; his mercies never come to an end!" Such a discordant shift in speech is found throughout the psalms of lament and serves to offset the rhetoric of complaint. The DV proceeds in a similar vein through v. 39. The placement of this normative voice in the center of the poem, as well as the poem's placement in the center of the book, suggests a conscious attempt to ideologically centralize the DV's theological position. As such it acts as a counterbalance not only to the first twenty-one verses of its own chapter, but also to the first two chapters of the book. The inclusion of a traditional DV in Lamentations serves to mitigate the rebellious wrath of Daughter Zion's complaint. It is essentially the intrusion of divine discourse into what is otherwise theologically troubling human speech.

> The Lord is good to those
> who wait for him,
> to the *nefesh* who seeks him.
> It is good that one should wait quietly
> for the salvation of the Lord. (Lam 3:25–26)

A focus on the juxtaposition of complaint and praise in a traditional lament highlights the way in which the poet of Lam 1–2 strove to say something new about his particular situation. In Lam 1–2, the "objective" voice (although the voice is actually often quite impassioned), the voice of authority, does not bother with defending God's righteousness, but rather puts all its weight behind Daughter Zion's complaint.

> YHWH determined to lay in ruins
> the wall of the daughter of Zion;

---

30. Tight structure may provide some order and boundary to devastating grief.

31. I am not much interested in issues of authorship or redaction, but the structural and theological discrepancies between Lam 1–2 and 3 makes reasonable the suggestion of many commentators that chapter 3 comes from a different hand than the Daughter Zion supplications.

> he marked it off by the line;
> he restrained not his hand from destroying . . . (Lam 2:8)

The DV expressly alludes to the two parties in contention (without parallel in the DV in the Psalms) and comes down clearly on the side of the supplicant. Newsom uses Lam 3 as a way to discuss Job's reconfiguring of the lament tradition, but her observations are equally illuminating for the way *bat Zion* reworks the lament.

> In Lamentations [3] the extensively described violence (Lam 3:1–20) serves as prelude to a word of hope (3:21), grounded in a conviction of the mercies of God (3:22–24). . . . Consequently, one should engage in self-examination and confession (3:40–42), drawing attention to one's suffering as motive for divine compassion (3:43–48). Job's act of resistance to this religiously sanctioned violence is to violate the form of the lament. At the point where the form invites reflection and confession, Job instead calls upon the earth itself not to cover his blood (Job 16:18). What the rhetoric of lament configured as legitimate punishment, Job . . . reconfigures as murder. The ravaged body serves not as the basis for compassionate appeal, as in Lam 3:43–48, but as the basis for accusation. (2003:137)

The call for self-reflection in Lam 3:40–42 finds no echo in the chapters that precede it. Even when the DV alludes to Daughter Zion's transgressions it comes across as no more than an aside, certainly not as denoting she deserves YHWH's choice of punitive response. Like Job, Zion's presentation of her ravaged body signifies a departure from the normative theology of lament. In contrast to Job, however, who has no defender, much of the effectiveness of Lam 1–2's reworking of the lament tradition comes from the redeployment of the DV, as much as from Zion's own presentation of her suffering.

It seems plausible to suggest that it is in part the influence of the city lament tradition in Mesopotamia that contributed to the poet's license in altering the rhetorical position of the DV. In both Lam 1–2 and the city laments, the "narrator's" function is to report on the deity's dealings with the city.

> Enlil afflicted the city with something that destroys cities,
> that destroys temples;
> He afflicted the city with something that cannot be withstood with
>     weapons;
> He afflicted the city with dissatisfaction and treachery.[32]

Still, the DV of Lamentations expresses itself in much less stylized and more personal, pathos-filled utterances, a quality that surely comes from an in-

---

32. Taken from P. Michalowski, *The Lamentations Over the Destruction of Sumer and Ur*, a composite text, lines 296–299.

digenous Israelite literary tradition, perhaps a combination of lament and
qinah, and perhaps inspired by a more democratic covenant tradition.[33]

To summarize the generic situation, both the lament psalms and Lam
1–2 are double-voiced poetry. They share features in the area of content as
well as structure. Attending to the formal and thematic features, however,
leads us to observe a major structural difference that has theological repercussions. While the supplicants' discourses are not substantially different
(Zion's may seem rather more harsh than most psalmic supplicants, but
note Ps 88 for an example of how close they can be), the discourse that
is generally characterized by third-person speech has essentially flipped
180 degrees. The function of the DV in the Psalms seems to be to defend
YHWH's goodness or justice, or, in a more pastoral sense, it might be understood as offering reassurance to the supplicant. In Lamentations, however,
one cannot discern a parallel function. The narrative voice understands
the supplicant's situation from her perspective, has seemingly internalized
her pain (and so, of course, in a sense could also be seen as performing a
pastoral function) (O'Connor 2002:107). What does it mean, theologically,
when the voice traditionally representing the divine position, the voice
of authority, speaks against its own interests and from the perspective of
suffering humans?[34]

The utter silence of God in Lam 1–2 suggests that the largely myopic
but consistent conviction that characterizes the discourse of the prophets
and DV in the Psalms dissolves into an inability to articulate a clear moral
and, by implication, theological judgment in Lam 1–2.

> What can I say for you,
> to what compare you, Daughter Zion?
> To what can I liken you,
> that I may comfort you, virgin Daughter Zion?
> For vast as the sea is your ruin;
> who can heal you? (2:13)

The DV of the Psalms, on the contrary, is never at a loss to respond to the
suffering of the supplicants. For them, God's governance of the universe is

---

33. In a private conversation (July 2004), Jerrold Cooper made the point that
in Mesopotamian literature there is little evidence that the gods were in direct
relationship with the people; rather, it is the king that features in any discussion
of human-divine relationality. "An amorous and conjugal relationship between
a nation as a collective and its deity is without parallel in the Ancient Near East.
The singularity of the marriage metaphor is best explained as a reflection of the
equally unique covenant concept that regulates the relationship between Yhwh
and Israel" (Abma: 23).

34. J. Scott speaks of the disproportionate impact elites wield when they
stand up against the very system that has supported their interests: "[T]hose ren-
egade members of the dominant elite who ignore the standard script . . . present a
danger far greater than their miniscule numbers might imply" (67).

in complete alignment with human notions of justice. Look, for example, at Ps 37, which I have elsewhere characterized as one long Didactic Voice. It seems composed to assuage every lament ever voiced.

> Fret not yourself because of the wicked,
> be not envious of wrongdoers,
> for they will soon fade like the grass,
> and wither like the green herb.

> YHWH knows the days of the blameless,
> and their heritage will abide forever;
> they are not put to shame in evil times,
> in the days of famine they have abundance. (Ps 37:1–2, 18–19)

Such speech seems conceived to respond precisely to every supplication ever made, but in Lamentations such a response is not to be found. Imagining the juxtaposition of this psalm with Daughter Zion's speech—

> Look, YHWH, and consider!
> To whom have you done this?
> Should women eat the fruit of their womb,
> the children they have borne? (Lam 2:20)

> Trust in YHWH, and do good;
> dwell in the land, and enjoy security. (Ps 37:3)

—makes it patently clear how inappropriate the typical DV would seem in the context of Lamentations. Confronted with Zion's perspective on God's justice, Ps 37's DV would come across as haughty disregard for her suffering and would set up a situation of irreconcilable dissonance for those living her words.

In the same way that the creator of *Wicked* preserves the signifiers of Elphaba by which she had traditionally been epitomized as evil, the poet of Lam 1–2 preserves the metaphor of Israel as a woman, a metaphor that in the discourse of the prophets is meant to humiliate and dehumanize the people, and imbues it with pathos and subjectivity. Elphaba is still green, Israel is still the adulterous wife, but no one who finally hears their story from their own mouths can make the same easy moral assessments that were possible when their stories were shaped only within the discourse of the Wizard and God, respectively.

The gap between God and Daughter Zion in this text may seem nearly unbridgeable, but, of course, this is only one moment in an ongoing relationship. The very fact that Zion cries out her anger attests to a future for the two.

> [C]omplaint . . . reaffirms the radically relational nature of the divine-human relationship that undergirds biblical faith. . . . In one respect, complaint is the lifeblood of the biblical notion of covenant: it ensures that the relationship is alive, dynamic, and open. Here faith is real, contested, actively negotiated. (Dobbs-Allsopp 2002:38)

The terror and incomprehensibility of her situation compels Zion to try to find language within her generic traditions to account for what has happened by countering and navigating the prophetic language that ostensibly already provides a rationale for her experience. The traditional account is no longer tenable in the culmination of what it prophesied. She constructs an alternative story, more authentic to her experience, by drawing on the language of lamentation, combined with elements of city lament and dirge (which contributes meter, vocabulary, and tone). Because the DV is the one place in the lament psalms that most logically lines up with the divine position of the prophets, it is that piece that must be swayed to her point of view so that her lament can resonate better in its particular context. The reorientation of the DV is a significant component in Zion's counterstory. It is particularly effective because the DV is traditionally recognized as a voice of the master narrative and so gives Zion's counterstory the credibility it would otherwise lack in the face of authority.[35]

Lamentations 1–2 transforms the language of the lament psalms and wrests the DV over to her point of view.[36] Zion does what the psalmic supplicants could or would not—she silences the divine/didactic voice. God is utterly silent in these two chapters as are his typical defenders.[37] Insofar as the traditional DV can only articulate the normative position, as often articulated in the prophetic accusations, it has no place in this poetry; the "party line" of the DV/prophetic voice would impose a nearly unbearable dissonance in this context. This modification to the lament provides Zion with a fitting response to the accusations leveled against her in the prophets through their deployment of the marriage metaphor. It further serves to emphasize how far apart husband and wife have become (before a move toward reconciliation is attempted in Second Isaiah). In a patriarchal context of honor and shame the marriage metaphor is a potent and effective rendering of God and Zion's troubled relationship in the Prophets. It constructs a discursive world in which the people's actions are construed as morally reprehensible, and without defense. Absent the imaginative world created by the metaphor, the "disloyalty" of Israel is rendered morally ambiguous. Outside of rigid YHWHism, polytheism simply does not equal adultery. The metaphor both conceals and reveals the dirty secret

---

35. H. Nelson says "counterstories can be created *by* or *for* the person whose identity needs repair" (19).

36. N. Lee notes this same dynamic vis-à-vis Jeremiah's empathetic response to Jerusalem's pain (61, 88).

37. Dobbs-Allsopp notes that God's silence is all the more curious because the god of the city laments does speak more often (2002:150). Enlil in The Lamentation over the Destruction of Sumer and Ur speaks often and offers a "friendly word." YHWH offers no word let alone a friendly one. Thus, this silence is either an intentional one, or merely reflects the relative silence of God in the lament psalms.

of biblical notions of identity formation—as Zion's desire should be re-
stricted to her husband, the people's should be to their god. R. Schwartz
chronicles the way in which many biblical texts contribute to an ideology
of "scarcity" (of land, love, blessings, and even the divine), a notion that
sets people against one another and moreover forces them to construct
their identities in opposition to the "other." The prophetic texts in question
contribute to this phenomenon (which still resonates tragically in today's
world), and rarely do biblical scholars (even feminist scholars) challenge
the assumptions of monotheism.[38]

---

38. As Kwok Pui-Lan notes, postcolonial readings of the Bible will (or should)
take care not to leave the Bible's "religious episteme intact" (139–40). In other
words, too often interpreters, even "progressive" ones, fail to challenge the Bible's
bias against "pagan" religions.

# 4

# Daughter Zion Finds Her Voice

*The centre cannot hold . . .* (W. B. Yeats, "The Second Coming")

*Every devil I meet is an angel in disguise.*[1] (Amy Ray of the Indigo
Girls)

## Introduction

In the prophetic texts that were the focus of chapter 2, Daughter Zion's
subjectivity is severely constrained by YHWH's rhetorical construction of
her. In chapter 3, I examined how the lament genre was reconfigured as a
partial response to the prophets. In this chapter I examine how the woman
reconfigures the prophets' own words to construct a counterstory that better reflects her experiences from her point of view. Among the questions
to be addressed is, how does Zion in Lam 1–2 repudiate specific charges
and rebut the divine "master narrative" as it is inscribed in the prophetic
marriage metaphor? Diamond and O'Connor urge us to listen for a point
of view other than the prophetic.

> The metaphor weaves a narrative in which the monologue of the injured
> husband alone is our source of information about this marriage. As often
> happens in divorce, it may be that the husband exaggerates the crimes
> of his spouse, blames her for everything wrong in the relationship, and
> makes as a condition of her return her acceptance of that blame. We hear
> him interrogate her belligerently and accuse her with his version of her
> words. . . . What would happen if female Israel told the story? Would

---

1. Lyrics from the song "Jonas and Ezekial." The names Jonas and Ezekial
were those of slaves, carved on gravestones. The song, according to Amy Ray, is
"a political song about people who put their faith in prophesy, who're walking
toward disaster instead of doing anything about it" (from a Web site devoted to
Indigo Girls trivia).

she tell of her husband's verbal abuse, his foolish jealousy, his despicable exaggerations. . . . (309–10)

What would happen, indeed . . . Both Lam 1 and 2 offer a psychological progression from the objective third-person voice of the DV to the passionate first-person voice of Zion herself (Kaiser: 174). Even in Lam 2, where the DV's discourse is marked by such intense pathos that it is hard to imagine Zion matching it, Zion's discourse ratchets up the intensity when she hurls accusations at the murderer of her children. The purpose of this chapter is not, however, to systematically show how Zion repudiates every charge leveled against her in the prophets. Rather, I am interested in showing compelling connections between the two discourses, connections that suggest an intentionality. Although I do not think it is far-fetched to read Lam 1–2 as a "response," in a chronological sense, to the prophetic discourses (especially Jeremiah) that construct Zion as a "sinner" and "whore," that is not so much my interest. There are theological gains to be made through a synchronic dialogical juxtapositioning of these discourses. It would be useful in this regard to keep in mind Juliana Claassen's mandate for biblical theology in a postmodern age: The task for biblical theology as she sees it is "to bring the diversity of voices within the biblical text into a dialogue" (133). Steven Kepnes, in his work on Buber, claims that a dialogical hermeneutics *requires* that we listen to the diversity of voices in and interpretations of biblical texts, and that we converse about them, in order to judge their merits (78). It is not necessary that the voices follow up on or respond to one another chronologically (Kepnes: 135–36). It is simply incumbent on us, as readers, to air those voices that have received little play until now. This is not to advocate a willy-nilly linkage of texts that have no inherent connection. We must be mindful that there are some logical connections inherent in the texts we bring into contact (Kepnes: 137).

Having stated that caveat, in this chapter I focus on Jeremiah and Ezekiel explicitly—two prophets that I maintain (with others, such as Hillers: xxii) have some temporal proximity and lexical connections to Lamentations. Another caveat might be in order. I am making no claims about gendered authorship. Although it is true that there was a tradition of female lamentation, and while it would be interesting and could have an impact on my interpretive claims if Zion were indeed a creation of an ancient Israelite woman, it is impossible to know and not really necessary for an assessment of the rhetorical interplay that exists between this voice (a "female" voice) and the divine/prophetic voice.[2]

It would be useful to lay out a few of the ways that counterstories do their work before we proceed. Nelson tells us that counterstories "ordinarily proceed by filling in details that the master narrative has ignored or

---

2. See William Lanahan, "The Speaking Voice in the Book of Lamentations," for an examination of Zion's voice as a female "persona" written by a male poet.

underplayed. Through augmentation and correction, the master narrative is *morally* reoriented, thus allowing the counterstory teller to dissent from the interpretation and conclusion it invites" (Nelson: 8, emphasis mine).[3] This is just common sense. We have all been in situations in which stories are circulating about us—even essentially harmless ones—that we do not think get the "facts" right. Our first instinct is to retell the story, filling in those ingredients that the original story failed to furnish, or stressing those aspects of the story that will make sense of our actions as they occur in the story. If we are convincing, we may be successful in restructuring the impression originally established in the minds of those who heard the different versions. Of course, we may not be successful. The audience may conclude that the facts of the original story better correspond to what they know about us, or they may simply trust the original speaker more than us. Cultural master narratives may influence their assessment as well. A given master narrative may have something to say about the way "people like us" do things and, depending on how controlling the particular master narrative is, it may be nearly impossible for people to reassess their take on our identity. The notion of master narrative is echoed in a similar concept described by C. Newsom as "iconic narrative."

> Iconic narratives encode fundamental commitments, social roles, and profiles of virtue that constitute the community. These narratives make meaningful—and therefore possible—certain forms of action. (2002:122)

For our purposes, then, the iconic narrative in the prophets is the script in which God and Zion are spouses and in which Zion betrays God, thereby justifying violent retribution. The metaphor is iconic because it both encodes and reflects several of Israel's ideological commitments—political, theological, and gendered.

Zion's power to reshape the impression of her given in the Prophets is limited, largely because she is trying to reshape *God's* story. By definition, any master narrative that the god of the text controls is going to assume nearly unassailable authority.[4] This rhetorical reality may be reflected by Zion's apparently rather limited goal of repudiating the prophetic discourse rather than positively crafting a new self-identity. It makes sense, though, that this would be the first step for anyone presenting a counterstory. In other words, she does not exactly tell a *new* story, but rather *reacts* to the terror God's story is responsible for inflicting on her.[5] Of course,

---

3. O'Connor notes that when Daughter Zion finds her voice in Lamentations, she recovers her life and acquires moral agency (2002:83).

4. Many postcolonial feminist theorists, including Spivak, recognize the difficulty of dislodging hegemonic discourses, of allowing a space for "subaltern" voices. See also M. Dube.

5. K. O'Connor borrows the term "narrative wreckage" from Arthur Frank. The term alludes to the "wreckage of one's life story that accompanies the discov-

there is no way to judge, in historical terms, Zion's success at subverting God's story, in other words, the effect she has on the world "behind the text."[6] What we can say, and what I hope to demonstrate, is that on the synchronic level she has altered the atmosphere of the world "of the text," and thus potentially the world "before the text." But because our master narratives are far more influenced by the prophet's point of view, it takes some special effort to "hear" Zion's counterstory, never mind to let it affect our master narratives. My task then is to help her tell her story by applying emancipatory reading strategies to illuminate aspects of her discourse that otherwise get pushed into the background by more conventional reading practices. R. Abma and other feminist critics make reading of this sort a moral imperative: Interpretation of "biblical texts [that] reflect asymmetrical gender patterns" that do not "expose the gender bias of such role patterns" have the effect of "authorizing and legitimating these patterns" (26). While this study has goals beyond purely feminist, the prophetic presentation of Israel as a woman and wife, as well as its echo in powerfully subversive language of Lam 1–2, requires that readers of these texts share the basic goals of feminist criticism, which as it turns out has an essential affinity with our focus on counterstories.

> A primary task of feminist criticism, therefore, is to investigate critically the way female characters function in the biblical texts. This is necessary in order to assess the way biblical writings reflect and support systems in which women are defined in relation to and from the perspective of men, as objects and victims rather than as independent and free creatures. (Abma: 26)

Spivak takes this injunction farther by contradicting it to some degree, but in a way I approve and employ in this study. The deconstructive task described above only really becomes a feminist reading when the category of *woman* is no longer hermeneutically objectified. Rather, the feminist deconstructivist must ask: "What is man that the itinerary of his desire creates such a text?" (191). In this way, woman can be restored to the position of the questioning subject. Y. Sherwood shares this concern and in her book

---

ery that one has a catastrophic illness." One's story about oneself is over, and a new story has yet to take its place (2002:7). Zion's story has undergone a similar wreckage both at the hands of the Babylonians and at the violent words leveled at her by YHWH's prophets. She obviously has not established a new story (although Second Isaiah is trying to construct one for her), so all she has for the moment is to blast away at the violence done to her, to contend against the story she did not choose for herself.

6. Although I think we can safely say that she does not seriously affect the forces supporting Israel's master narrative—patriarchy and exclusive monotheism as the only morally acceptable religious practice are even to this day alive and well. This accords with L. Gandhi's admission that the "post-" of postcolonialism should not lead us to expect a definitive break with the colonial past (7).

on Hosea deconstructs the subject-object dichotomy, which objectifies the feminine, and challenges feminist criticism, which often (even if unwittingly) cooperates in that objectification (1996). The text of Lam 1–2 leads us in this direction naturally. We are induced to read *with* Daughter Zion and *toward* God/male as object, thus automatically restoring the woman to a subject position, rather than the object position in which most feminist practice traps her.

Through the use of the first- and second-person discourse, we get the impression of Zion telling God "to his face" that his story is not the whole story. Zion's attempt (as well as our own) to reorient the moral assessment with which the prophetic story paints her fits Nelson's understandings of counterstories as "narrative acts of insubordination" in that through her recapitulation of the prophetic discourse from her point of view she naturally challenges not only the (patriarchal, monotheistic, retributive) worldview that many Israelites surely shared (including Zion, apparently), but also challenges God's presentation of himself (8). By juxtaposing those prophetic texts that represent YHWH as speaking directly to the woman with Lam 1–2, we are able to put together something very close to an actual dialogue.[7] Our heuristic construction of a moral encounter between these particular texts allows us to address many ethical and theological questions, especially those that most interest readers with feminist, postcolonial, and liberation concerns. Of course, we have learned the advantages of putting a wide array of biblical texts into dialogue with one another (as well as with extrabiblical texts), but these texts are particularly propitious conversation partners for establishing a dialogic theology. The opportunity to examine the actual speech of the players we are interested in understanding better is an invaluable opportunity—just as a psychotherapist commissioned with the task of helping a couple better understand their relationship insists on staging situations in which she can listen to the partners talk to each other in order to uncover where they miscue, why trust is lacking, and so on. In this study, there is, of course, much more than a single relationship at play. The marriage metaphor opens up onto bigger worlds and bigger stakes. First, it figures the relationship between YHWH and his people Israel; second, it bears on contemporary relationships between humans (not least women and men), and humans and God, especially those humans who have been directly shaped to some degree or other by the biblical tradition. In short, the marriage metaphor constitutes

---

7. Of course on the ethical level this calls to mind Lévinas's injunction that ethics be based on the face-to-face encounter with the "Other." F. Fanon, the postcolonial psychoanalyst, also insisted that freedom from oppression must begin here: "In particular Fanon emphasized the essentiality of *reciprocal recognition* for human life and relatedness. Without reciprocal recognition, there can be no identity, no self-worth, no dignity" (Bulhan: 114).

a master narrative on many levels, transcending time and even modes of signification.

The theological assumption behind the prophetic warnings and behind many readings of Lamentations, as well, is that Jerusalem is *justifiably* punished for her sins, that she is reaping what she sowed. Not surprisingly, most interpreters privilege the divine/prophetic discourse over that of the woman. Even in Lamentations—a book without the divine voice present—they interject it over the living voice of the text. Recently, many scholars have made some sorely needed corrections to this reading. There has been a flurry of fine commentaries and monographs on Lamentations—by T. Linafelt, K. O'Connor, A. Berlin, F. W. Dobbs-Allsopp (and C. Westermann, to some extent, before them)—which appropriately relieve Daughter Zion of some burden of guilt. Far more than was the case in the past, these scholars recapitulate Zion's exclamations of outrage toward a god who would allow, let alone sanction, such a calamity. To a greater or lesser degree, they note that the "message," the purpose of the book, is not Zion's acknowledgment of her sin, is not an attempt at repentance, is not meant to show the people the way back to their god, but rather is meant mostly as a emotional expression of existential pain, shock, and betrayal. Dobbs-Allsopp notes that the poems give a nod to the notion that sin is to blame, but insists that in the end a theodic reading of the book is a misreading (2002:29). In effect, practicing a dialogic hermeneutic, these exegetes give due weight to the (implicit) claims of the so-called "sinner," urging readers into more honest assessments of their understandings of the divine-human relationship.

Inspired by the work of a number of feminist scholars who have examined the social, rhetorical, and theological implications of the prophetic marriage metaphor, I want to foreground the prophets' construction of Zion as exactly that—a construction. This task was begun in chapter 2, but an examination of the way Zion constructs a counterstory will serve, by contrast, to further demonstrate the political nature of the prophets' portrait. To borrow from Bakhtin's dialogic terminology, God and the prophets "author" Zion irresponsibly. That is, there is no reciprocity in their construction. It is not that the strokes they use to paint her are false; it is rather that they are calculated to maintain a theological and social status quo and take no consideration of her point of view. Barbara Green explains it well when she says that "to author respectfully is to acknowledge the other with discipline, responsivity, and refinement, to negotiate rather than to bully" (2000:35–36). As in any healthy marriage, God and Zion need to learn the art of negotiation. Both need to listen more and talk less, but this is especially true of God. In Jer 8:6, YHWH claims to have "given heed and listened," but he did not like what he heard. Evidently, the only acceptable response from Zion would have been the admission and repentance of sin. This is something—in the Prophets at least—that

Jerusalem is apparently unwilling to do, but we are never given a chance to hear her side of the case. This is because, on an ideological level, the prophetic texts are largely monologic. Bakhtin says, "In a monologic work the ultimate and finalizing authorial evaluation of a character is, by its very nature, a *secondhand* evaluation, one that does not presuppose or take into account any potential *response* to this evaluation on the part of the character himself" (or in this case, herself) (1984:70). Human discourse is conspicuously absent from the Prophets, and when humans do speak it is speech that is (almost) always inflected through divine discourse and that is intended to serve divine ideological interests. The truth is that God does the opposite of authoring respectfully—he is a bully. Feminist and postcolonial theory speak to this assessment: One of the primary aims of feminism has been "to enable women to become the active participating subjects rather than the passive reified objects of knowledge" (Gandhi: 44). This is of course also true of those resisting colonialism: Said understands colonial discourse as the "cultural privilege of representing the subjugated Other" (Gandhi: 86). Thus, the act of resistance involves laying claim to one's subjectivity. In this regard, I find Daughter Zion the Bible's most intrepid female voice of resistance.

In Jer 6 and elsewhere, God accuses the people of not listening (Jer 6:10–11). This is undoubtedly true and suggests that humans are guilty of irresponsible authoring as well, or at least share in the breakdown of the marriage covenant. But the truth is that authoring never proceeds in a power-neutral way. Zion's words in Lamentations are influenced by the primacy of YHWH's discourse in a way that YHWH's words are not influenced by hers. Feminist and postcolonial theory has made this point again and again in the context of patriarchy and colonialism. Women and indigenous peoples are constructed by the words of those in power, and even when they use their own voice to speak, the dominator's words are all mixed in, to a greater or lesser degree, with their own words (Leclerc: 363). In this regard, an important critique of Bakhtin is that authoring rarely takes place on an even playing field: "A key issue among feminist and postcolonialist readers is the likelihood of a benign encounter between uneven voices. That is, Bakhtin's sense of authoring disregards power" (Green 1984:59). It can, in fact, be dangerous for the weaker of the dialogue partners to let the more powerful "other" inside. A dialogic theology that does not take seriously the inevitability of power discrepancies between uneven voices runs the risk of reinscribing the inequality of which monologic readings are guilty. While Bakhtin's sense of authoring seems to disregard power, that does not weaken the good work his dialogical approach can do toward evening out precisely such power disparities. In fact, the very foundation of Bakhtin's philosophy of alterity depends on the understanding of language as a living, evolving phenomenon, in which "past meanings always modify themselves (and renew themselves) in the unfolding of subsequent dialogue. It seems perfectly appropriate, therefore, that feminism should add its voice to this critical dialogue, with the aim of enriching with new meanings our understanding of Bakhtin and of feminist theories" (Hajdu-kowski-Ahmed: 154). As Ilana Pardes notes, although "the dominant thrust of the Bible is clearly patriarchal, patriarchy is continuously challenged by antithetical trends" (51). It is up to us to make women's words heard more clearly.

N. Gottwald, with his interest in reading biblical texts in terms of (Marxist) sociological categories, notes that most literature developed under a tributary mode of production (an economic system shared by most of the ancient Near East, and certainly true of the Persian Empire), "is produced to satisfy state administrative and ideological needs" (45). I find the claim that most biblical texts were produced by a political elite to advance particular explicit and implicit agendas compelling, overall. In the case of Lamentations, however, it is difficult to imagine what kind of elitist agenda the text might be promoting. It could be the protest of a relatively elite class that remained in Judah after the deportations and felt that the loss of its power was an injustice. In that case it would be right to consider it ideologically aimed at restoring a lost status quo, except that there are several places in the text that profess a disillusionment with Judah's leaders (Gottwald: 47). If, indeed, Lamentations is the product of the very elite that the prophets lambaste for their acts of idolatry and social crimes, it would militate against the kind of emancipatory reading I am propos-ing. The speaker in the text might instead come across as hypocritical and unworthy of sympathy. But because it is fairly definite that Lamentations was written in Judah and not by displaced Judean elites, and because the text is constructed as the grievance of a people figured as a marginalized woman (a disgraced and unclean woman, no less), the text, regardless of the status of its progenitors, lends itself to emancipatory interpretive aims. The speaker's report of her experience of unsurpassable horror and depri-vation puts the text in a good position to speak to those who have suffered state-sponsored terror, specifically, as well as the oppression of master nar-ratives, generally.

Finally, I make the admittedly provocative claim that Lam 1–2 is less ideological and tendentious than the prophetic texts. Ideology as a con-cept is notoriously difficult to pin down, but I accept J. Berquist's broad understanding as a working definition: Ideology refers to "patterned human discourse that privileges those persons in power who initiate that discourse" (25). I would nuance this only by saying that the ideological hi-erarchies alluded to here exist within many institutions, so we do not need to think only of ultimate (state or divine) power (although in the discursive world inhabited by the marriage metaphor I think we are). The discursive hegemony of the powerful renders their discourses "natural" and self-evident. Zion, configured as a shamed woman by prophetic discourse, is the ultimate embodiment of powerlessness. As such, her speech is confronted with a rhetorical uphill battle. Her discourse is not "patterned" in support of powerful impulses, but is rather a discourse of resistance against those very impulses. Another way of putting it is to read Zion's rhetoric as more personal than political, and therefore lacking in cultural determining power. So when, for lack of a better term, I refer to Zion's "ideology," it is in the general sense of worldview or symbolic point of view.

## Application

The following analysis consists of intertextual readings between Hosea, Jeremiah, and Ezekiel and Lam 1–2. More attention will be paid to Jeremiah and Ezekiel than Hosea, in part because of their many lexical and historical connections to Lamentations.

The notion that the prophetic marriage metaphor is being invoked, at least implicitly, in the Book of Lamentations has support in the comparable Mesopotamian city laments in which the city is personified (deified) as the patron god's spouse. Internally, the city is referred to as an *'almanah* ("widow") in Lam 1:1. As my reading tries to demonstrate, Zion is called a widow because she has been abandoned by her divine husband, as well as by the death of her human family.[8] Dobbs-Allsopp also sees a connection between Lamentations and the marriage metaphor and begins to read in the direction I want to go:

> It may be assumed, insofar as the poem is culturally situated in a context where adultery is defined asymmetrically in terms of the rights of the husband as head of the household, that the poet [of Lamentations] means to tap into the motif's cultural symbolism.[9] (2002:63–64)

There are, however, significant alterations in the rhetoric that shift the blame away from the culpability of Zion and toward issues of suffering.

### Hosea's Idealism

As one might expect, Hosea, unlike Jeremiah and Ezekiel, finds little direct echo in Lam 1–2. In any case, I showed in chapter 2 how Hosea does a pretty good (although unintentional) job himself of deconstructing his ac-

---

8. See N. Graetz, "Jerusalem the Widow," for the way the rabbis nuance the understanding of "widow." They note that she is "like" a widow (otherwise it would mean God is dead!), that God is no longer acting like a husband, but that unlike a real widow, she is not free to remarry, either.

9. There is not space here to rehearse all the arguments for supporting a connection between the Prophets and Lamentations through the employment of the marriage metaphor, but Kathleen O'Connor has done just that (1999a:282). While she briefly charts the marriage metaphor as it journeys from the earlier prophets to Lamentations in order finally to discuss Second Isaiah's reception of Daughter Zion rhetoric, I stay focused on the connections between the earlier prophets and Lamentations.

cusations against the woman and exposing YHWH's vulnerability. In short, there just is not as much "fire" there to which Zion might need to respond as there is in the other two prophets; those passages in Hosea that do cry out for response are, for the most part, echoed in Jeremiah and Ezekiel. The one aspect of Hosea's use of the marriage metaphor that I would like briefly to address and that does not find a close parallel in Jeremiah and Ezekiel is the section at the end of Hos 2 in which the deity re-betroths the woman to him. At several points in Hos 2:16–25, the rhetoric focuses on interpersonal communication—between the deity and the woman, the deity and the cosmos, the cosmos and the earth: "I will speak coaxingly to her . . ." (v. 16); ". . . she shall respond as in the days of her youth" (v. 17); "You will call me *'ishi*" (v. 18); "I will respond to the sky and it will respond to the earth" (v. 23); and so on. In contrast, because of the way woman is systematically omitted in the preceding passages, the move toward dialogic engagement would appear to be promising. As pointed out in chapter 2 of this study, however, YHWH's overtures are altogether one-sided; he is still up to his old tricks of discursively constituting Zion: "she will respond"; "you will call me"; "I will sow her." In other words, he cannot stop "playing god." Zion's words, absent YHWH's mediation, are not represented. The nearest we have to a response occurs at the end of the chapter when YHWH says of *Lo-ammi*: "And he will say, '[you are] my god.'" Note, however, that the respondent has been converted to a male voice so that the impression conveyed is that only males are worthy of the (near) autonomy of expressing their desires. As we saw with Ezekiel, prophecy of reconciliation tends to feature God and male figures, exclusively.

The rhetoric of hope is couched in eschatological terms, which is understandable if Hosea's prophecy was recorded when many assume it was, near to the devastation of 721 B.C.E. Sadly, the prophecy did not come to pass; the Israelites were not again heard from as a cohesive group. The Judahites, ultimately, preserved this prophecy as it spoke so well to their experience of eventual return to Judah. Whatever the historical reality, however, rhetorically we are not given a glimpse of this dialogically fulfilling future. The closest we may come is Second Isaiah, but, as we will see, even there YHWH's primary purpose is to reconstitute Zion's identity into one that once again trusts him to "comfort" her, whether the trust is warranted or not. In the interim, Lam 1–2 does not record any such dialogue. Not only does God not speak "tenderly" to Zion, but she is far from referring to him as *'ishi*. In fact, YHWH does not answer her emotive rhetoric at all, and Zion seems to give up on any chance of real dialogue. YHWH's (lovely) illusion of his and his wife's communing heart to heart is not realized in Hosea, nor in any of the Prophets, nor is it realized in Lamentations. Past Genesis, in fact, we do not have any kind of communication between deity and human that comes close to what YHWH foresees in Hosea. Why doesn't the Bible include more instances of genuine divine-human interaction? Perhaps it is simply a reflection of the ontological divide between embodiment and transcendence? Whatever the case, it is troubling that even YHWH is not portrayed as being able to overcome it.[10] Without a doubt, it is an important question to ponder for a dialogic theology and one that haunts this study. Jeremiah and Ezekiel are less idealistic and more cynical, but their rhetoric does make more sense of the tension we encounter in Lam 1–2.

*Jeremiah and the Rhetoric of Guilt and Innocence*

Jeremiah 2 begins with YHWH reminiscing nostalgically about Jerusalem as his "once upon a time" bride (2:3). But the honeymoon is short-lived when the people (now portrayed as males) stray from their god, never even bothering to ask, "Where is YHWH?" (2:6, 8). After a description of "his" (i.e., Israel's) cities laid waste (2:15), the rhetoric returns to female figuration in order to accuse the woman of bringing this devastation on Israel. Structurally, however, something insidious is going on. "She" is accused of causing "his" (male Israel's) devastation: "This [i.e., destruction of *male* Israel's cities] is what your [f.s.] forsaking YHWH your [f.s.] God is doing to you [f.s.]" (2:17). In other words, *she* deserves what *he* gets. While in translation the pronouns do not register clearly, for ancient audiences the switch from male to female would have been marked. The form of this rhetoric subtly establishes a portrait of the woman as heartless and calculating and as the source of male destruction. Of course, as we know, she will share in their destruction, and then some. But this initial rhetorical situation supports the view that she doubly deserves what she gets for being the source of the trouble. Jeremiah has not yet used the word "whore" (*zonah*) to describe the woman, but this initial salvo effectively sets the stage. In Lamentations, Zion readily concedes that "they" did indeed suffer immeasurably, but her counterstory is infused with pathos as she makes it clear that "they" are *her* beloved children: "my young men" (Lam 1:15); "my children" (Lam 1:16); "my young women and my young men" (Lam 1:18; 2:21); "my people" (Lam 2:11); not to mention the passages in which the people are similarly referred to by the DV.[11] The identity she crafts for herself is that of the victimized woman and bereft mother in contrast to the villain of Jeremiah's "narrative." In this, Daughter Zion significantly shifts the focus of the metaphor as construed in the Prophets, where the focus was on Zion as wife. Zion morally reorients the rhetoric by focusing on herself as bereaved nurturer. In this discourse, she is first and foremost a mother, not

---

10. This is obviously one of the tensions the Christian doctrine of the incarnation is trying to resolve.

11. Barbara Bakke Kaiser notes how the poet moves into the female "persona" when "he's" going for the greatest emotional impact: "[T]he poet begins with a third-person narrator but changes to the female persona at the point of greatest tension; that is, the poet chooses the female persona to express the intensity of his grief" (166).

a wife—a self-description that eschews the sexualization of her identity in
the Prophets. (As we see in the next chapter, in discussion of Second Isaiah,
YHWH attempts to paint himself with the same maternal strokes.)

Alongside the aspects of Israel's patriarchal narrative just noted, another master narrative is evoked in this section of Jeremiah—the idea of
a "doctrine of retribution." That is, the text evokes the notion that suffering is a direct result of and in proportion to the crimes committed: "Your
wickedness will punish you, and your backsliding rebuke you" (Jer 2:19).
Deuteronomistic writings are rife with tales of and laws enjoining ostensibly deserved retribution, but the doctrine is found in a diversity of biblical
genres (and is, in fact, alive if not so well, in contemporary Western culture).
It seems to have been an ideology that had enormous cultural influence,
but one that because of its rigidity could be exposed as false by experiences (personal or political) that did not conform to its simplistic notions of
causality. However, because the doctrine of retribution was ideologically
fundamental and insisted on the comforting notion that order triumphs
over chaos and that all suffering is earned, evidence of its shortcomings
would be hard to swallow, even by those parties with the most reason
to doubt it. And when the weaknesses of powerful master narratives are
made apparent, "serious amounts of confusion and bad faith" result for the
members of the community for which it held sway (Nelson: 133). Texts like
Job, Ps 88, and Lamentations attest to this capacity for "bad faith" against
the backdrop of these ideological tensions. In short, Zion (like Job) knows
that the doctrine of retribution, strictly speaking, is a specious notion, and
much of her counternarrative is aimed first and foremost at disabusing her
audience of the idea that YHWH always acts in perfect accord with the rule
of just deserts. On the violence that master or iconic narratives, such as the
doctrine of retribution, can do to "truth," Newsom asks:

> Are such configurations of the imagination that impose "narrative con-
> sonance . . . on temporal dissonance" a form of treachery, a "violence of
> interpretation"? Do they "tell a story" in the sense of a lie? (2003:134)

The naive equation of guilt and suffering presented by the prophets just
doesn't add up. It is a "lie" perpetrated for the not altogether ignoble purpose of rendering otherwise meaningless violence meaningful.

YHWH's charges become more specific when, according to YHWH,
through the prophet, Jerusalem breaks her yoke and declares, "I will not
serve!" (2:20), starts "playing the whore" by spreading her legs for every
Tom, Dick, and Baal (2:23), "sniffing the wind" (or "panting") like a wild ass
in heat (2:24). Jerusalem has become so degenerate that she can even teach
the "wicked women" a trick or two (2:33).[12] While Jeremiah condemns the

---

12. In addition to fornication, Jerusalem's skirts are stained with the life-
blood of the "innocent poor" (2:34). Parenthetically, one observation might shed
light on the reference in Lam 1:9 to the "uncleanness" in Zion's skirts: contrary to

woman for breaking out of her yoke (Jer 2:20), Daughter Zion speaks from
a position still firmly under YHWH's yoke.

> The yoke of my rebellion is bound fast,
> lashed tight by his hand,
> imposed upon my neck,
> it saps my strength. (Lam 2:14ab)

The connotations of "yoke" vary considerably between Jeremiah and Lam
1–2. For the prophet, being bound is the preferable state, while for Daughter Zion YHWH's yoke is an unfavorable imposition, but one that seemingly
cannot be broken (in spite of Jeremiah's assertion). Contrary to the apparent preference of many translations, פשע ("rebellion") should not be
understood as referring to "transgressions" or "offenses" in the sense
of "sins," per se. It often has a political edge to it, as when nations rebel
against nations (see Amos 1:3, 6, 9, 11, 13). Thus, even when it has to do
with rebellion against God, as it does here, it lacks the moral connotations
of other terms, such as עון. In Jer 13:22, God says bluntly that "it is for the
greatness of your sins [root עון] that your skirts are lifted up, that you are
sodomized [lit., your backside/buttocks treated violently]" (Jer 13:22). In
other words, it is YHWH's position that her terrorization is a direct result of
her immoral behavior. Thus, it is worth noting that Zion does not herself
use עון when referring to her own transgressions. From an ancient Near
Eastern perspective, the rebellion of a subservient party—often a vassal
nation against the powers that be—might legitimately be met with harsh
reprisals, but contemporary readers may naturally laud the struggles of
the weak against the strong. In the same way that she does not deny taking lovers, Zion does not deny rebelling against God. This should not
be understood as a confession of sin, however, but rather as merely an
acknowledgment that the stronger party has taken action against her rebellion and prevailed.

According to YHWH, Zion's escape from bondage to him involves getting
cozy with others, in essence "serving" other gods (Jer 2:20b), an illicit activity that renders her irreversibly unclean (Jer 2:22). In Jeremiah, YHWH implies
that she denies both the charge of adultery and its result: "How can you say,
'I am not unclean; I have not gone after the Baalim'?" In Lamentations, she
does not deny the charge of taking other lovers, but the language of defilement has no place in her counterstory. In Lam 1:9, the "narrator" makes
reference to the "uncleanness" in her skirts, but it makes sense to read this
as a result of the invasion of "her sanctuary" by the nations (Lam 1:10), those
previously forbidden entry because of purity requirements. In any case, in
none of Zion's own speech does the issue of uncleanness come up in re-

---

the belief of many scholars that the uncleanness refers to menstruation, it is more
likely a reference to bloodshed or, as A. Berlin (54) and K. O'Connor (1999b:22)
think, sexual relations.

gards to her condition. In fact, if anyone is at fault for causing defilement it is
YHWH himself, for he has slaughtered "priest and prophet in the sanctuary of
the Lord" (Lam 2:20c). Zion's implicit rebuttal of the accusation of uncleanness can also be construed as a retort against the charge in Ezek 23:38–39,
whereby she is accused of defiling the temple by sacrificing her children and
entering the temple on the same day. Strangely, though, after YHWH presents
her with the evidence of her insatiable, bestial sexual appetite, she concedes
the partial truth of his claim and announces: "It is hopeless, for I have loved
strangers, and after them I will go" (Jer 2:25). We have already rehearsed
other translation options (ch. 2), but an additional option is that since this
claim follows YHWH's presentation of damning evidence, she might simply
mean by "it is hopeless" that there is no longer any point in denying the
charges. We have already seen her admit to lovers in Lam 1.

In any case, no matter how we translate or interpret, it seems clear
that YHWH is trying to demonstrate Zion's shamelessness. This accusation
is countered, however, by YHWH's next quotation. At the end of a long list
of allegations, God cites Jerusalem as announcing, "I am innocent" (Jer
2:35a). As noted in chapter 2, this proclamation, more than anything else,
seems to enrage the deity. His immediate response is: "Now I am bringing
you to judgment for saying 'I have not sinned'" (2:35b). Punishment is, in
other words, a direct consequence of a self-assessment contrary to divine
assessment. The combination of admission and denial of guilt suggests a
reality somewhere between: Zion has lovers, but this does not mean she is
"guilty." Already in the Prophets—despite their extreme monologism—we
catch a glimpse of the woman's attempt to counter YHWH's narrative of her.
YHWH's harsh response to this in Jeremiah supports Nelson's claim that
resistance to master narratives frequently results in an even stronger insistence on the normative story line. Oftentimes the stronger the evidence to
the contrary, the greater the backlash:

> Pictures created by master narratives are so strongly resistant to evidence
> because what they say about certain groups of people is only common
> sense, what everybody knows, what you don't have to think about,
> what's necessarily the case. . . . [D]isconfirming instances tend to provoke
> a normative backlash. (Nelson: 148)

The direct linkage of punishment to her resistance of his characterization
may have profound implications for the way Zion addresses herself to
God in Lamentations. Despite her apparent refusal to acknowledge her
transgressions in Jeremiah, in Lam 1:18 she appears finally willing to con-
fess her crime: "The Lord is just, for I have rebelled against his word."
At least that is how many commentators read it—as a straightforward acknowledgment of sin, an act of repentance, even.[13] This is certainly a valid

---

13. Even Dobbs-Allsopp reads her confession as "genuine," although he does
not see it as the "soul" of the discourse. In *Weep O Daughter Zion: A Study of the*

reading, but perhaps not a complete reading. What Zion might be admitting to here is her failure to heed the word of the prophets (or at least the "true" prophets), a reading that aligns with the recognition in Lam 2:14 that at least some prophets misled her. In this, Zion is acknowledging to a certain extent her dialogic shortcomings.

Read in light of Jer 2:35, however, and with the awareness that divine words about her carry a disproportionate amount of discursive power, Zion's confession might be read as coerced. Coercion in this situation occurs because oppressive discourse "often infiltrates a person's consciousness, so that she comes to operate, from her own point of view, as her oppressors want her to, rating herself as they rate her" (Nelson: 7).[14] This is certainly a plausible reading of her confession given the enormous force master narratives exert on our consciousnesses:

> The teller of a counterstory is bound to draw on the moral concepts found in the master narratives of her tradition, since these played a key role in her moral formation regardless of how problematic her place within that tradition has been. . . . (Nelson: 67)

The evidence, however, seems to point away from self-recrimination, coerced or otherwise. Lexical, grammatical, and contextual factors converge to suggest a more ironic intent.[15] First, the Hebrew of v. 18 is ambiguous enough to warrant the suggestion that Zion is not admitting to "rebellion" at all. Rather than *mrh* (to rebel), it is possible to read מריתי from the root

---

*City-Lament Genre in the Hebrew Bible*, he states, "[O]ne could even gain the impression that the sin motif is almost perfunctory in nature. . . . Moreover, the poem implicitly and explicitly questions the appropriateness and degree of Yahweh's punishment" (2002:31, 54–64). Typical Jewish theology and liturgy interprets the exile as a response to sin (Graetz: 16), but there is plenty of midrash (e.g., *Lamentations Rabbah*) that takes God to task for the severity of his punishment.

14. Power is not simply an effect of the state's domination of the individual—or a result of one group or individual oppressing another. The state's power to produce a totalizing web of control is dependent on its ability to co-opt the individual's participation (Gandhi: 11, 14). Master narratives and myths exert this kind of influence. Some feminists argue that patriarchy is so discursively internalized in women that the road to liberation cannot be through the language patriarchy has constructed. Others, though, "suggest that the ambiguities of androcentric discourse allow for all kinds of creative possibilities" (Sherwood 1996:291). I locate myself primarily in the latter camp (I am dubious that there are other feasible options) but am very aware of the power androcentric discourse and master narratives exert, a power that is sometimes insurmountable.

15. Irony, in this case, evokes Bakhtin's notion of "excess vision," whereby Zion is able to see God and God's actions from a perspective that is inaccessible to him. Theologically, this has obvious difficulties, but seems rhetorically plausible. N. Lee senses that Daughter Zion is being "sarcastic" here (134).

*mrr* (to be bitter).[16] C. L. Seow has done precisely that with the exact same word in v. 20 (and A. Berlin accepts his amendment) (Seow: 416–19; Berlin: 44, 47). That מריתי occurs in two verses so near to one another, but with seemingly different intent, indicates that, at the very least, ambiguity was intended in this regard. (And if Naomi can be "embittered" by the loss of a husband and sons, why not Zion?) But because the effectiveness of irony usually requires a shared cultural context, we may not have the ears to hear Zion's claim of YHWH's justice in v. 18 as satirical, so we imagine she must be admitting to fault in this case. James Scott makes a fascinating case for the way subordinates manipulate the power relations in which they are involved, by going underground with their resistance—making their words ambiguous enough in public contexts that they cannot be held responsible for the negative implications of their speech. He calls this discursive resistance, which takes many different forms—the "hidden transcripts" of subordinates, as opposed to the "public transcript" that functions to maintain the rationale for social hierarchy. Heuristically, it is useful to read Lamentations as a type of hidden transcript. [17]

A more satirical, or "inflected," reading of this verse aligns with Bakhtin's understanding of double-voiced discourse, in which an "other's" words are recontextualized in one's speech and in the process the meaning of the speech is transformed (1984:189).

> In ordinary speech the words one speaks are always partly one's own and partly those of someone else. This phenomenon can buttress one's own speech by invoking the words and phrases associated with someone or some discourse the speaker treats as authoritative. Or it can undercut another position, as in parodic speech. In both cases the speaker's own accents as well as those of the other posited speaker are present and actively engaged in dialogic relationship. But the words of another sometimes appear in one's own speech in a nondialogical way. This is what Bakhtin refers to as the "authoritative word."[18] (Newsom 2003:28)

As has been demonstrated of all women situated in patriarchal discursive contexts, Zion cannot help but express herself through the language of the

---

16. N. Lee maintains *mrh*, but inflects it differently: "Innocent is YHWH, but I rebel against his speech!" (132).

17. To be more than merely heuristic help, we would have to know more about the situation of the poet and his or her relationship to the religious culture. Standard laments, such as those we find dominating in the Psalter, would fall into the category of public transcript, because although they also express protest, they "tow the line" for the most part, largely because of the influence of the Didactic Voice.

18. While the discourse that constructs Zion as a sinner definitely belongs to the authoritarian discourse of the deity, and thus might demand an admission of sin from Zion, it still seems reasonable to read her admission in a dialogic, almost parodic, manner; Zion is holding two positions in tension.

dominant discourse.[19] Still, it is hard to know whether Zion's "confession" should be read as derisive, or whether it is a straightforward acknowledgment of the authority from whence it originated. But whether Zion intends it or not, her use of YHWH's words does not straightforwardly reproduce the meaning YHWH intended. Even if she is uttering a confession we need not hear it as support for YHWH's actions. In fact, because these particular words (i.e., prophetic accusations) have affected her life so negatively, her relationship to them is necessarily going to be troubled. YHWH's words simply sound wrong in her mouth. Her struggle against the language of (prophetic) tradition resonates with Job's plight as Carol Newsom sees it. She notes that the friends have an easy relationship with the language and tradition from which they are drawing, while Job "picks his way through a shattered language that he can wield only in fragments" (2003:131). The prophets are understandably at home with the words they speak, since their words emanate from the source of their language tradition itself—in other words, they carry transcendent authority. In contrast, Daughter Zion struggles for coherence. Her words are fragmented and often contradictory, like Job's: "Though he does not struggle with language at the level of grammar, Job's attempt to express his own truth about the violence he has experienced ... requires him to dislocate and remold the words, metaphors, and genres through which traditional language had constructed a world of meaning" (Newsom 2003:131–32). Likewise, Daughter Zion recontextualizes the prophetic word to express her own truth about the violence she has experienced. *It is no longer possible to speak an easy truth about God's justice or meaningful existence.*

In any case, if a declaration of innocence serves no better purpose than getting her raped and her children slaughtered, it is no wonder that in Lamentations Zion abandons any notion of a straightforward counterattack and, instead, lets her words convey on multiple levels. This may account for the odd juxtaposition of admissions of guilt with scathing attacks on YHWH's justice. If she is indeed mocking him (albeit discreetly), Job chose to approach a similar situation in a quite different way. He persisted in proclaiming his innocence, even when he recognized that genuine reciprocity with God was impossible: "Though I am innocent, I cannot answer him. . . . If I summoned him and he answered, I do not believe that he would listen to my voice. . . . Though I am innocent, my own mouth would condemn me; though I am blameless, he would prove me perverse" (Job 9:15, 16, 20). What Job meant facetiously, Zion demonstrates literally: In Lam 1:9, her own mouth does condemn her. And in a (Deuteronomic?) prose insertion in Jer 3, YHWH says: "Yet for all this . . . Judah did not return to me with her whole heart, but only in pretense" (3:10). Whatever attempts she seems to have made toward returning are not accepted, just as Job predicts that

---

19. For a linguistic study that addresses this phenomenon, see R. Lakoff.

any case he might make for himself would have no effect on YHWH. In their discursive contexts, neither Job nor Zion wields any "cognitive authority." "As a number of feminist epistemologists have argued, cognitive authority is dependent on social position—it requires a certain standing within one's community" (Nelson: 172). In the biblical worldview, one's standing is dependent on acquiescence to God's authority and traditional theological precepts. In the Bible, cognitive authority rests largely, if not solely, with YHWH. YHWH's epistemological hegemony over Daughter Zion in particular is manifest in how he knows her, speaks for her, and even responds to the words he has spoken for her. This situation is illustrative of Foucault's concept of discourse as a system of regulation—in other words, those in power control knowledge (although not completely). Ironic, however, is that the use of a marriage metaphor actually mitigates YHWH's hegemony to some degree. In the prophetic texts focused on the marriage metaphor, God speaks as husband and lead covenant partner, rather than as a divine being. God assumes an axiological position vis-à-vis Zion that is as particular as any other subject's. In other words, like any person, God assigns specific values to Zion that are determined by his own ends. Biblical interpreters who give unqualified credence to YHWH's judgments do not seem to take this into account.

Jeremiah 4:30–31 also has a bearing on Lam 1:18. God, through the prophet, takes Daughter Zion to task for beautifying herself for her lovers, painting her eyes, and adorning herself in finery. The woman's crime is that she has asserted a right to independently choose her partners. She has forgotten her "proper place," that is, the place the master narrative has reserved for her (Brenner: 96). Jeremiah predicts that all her beautifying is for naught, because Zion's lovers hate her and seek her life. And in Lamentations we hear from Zion's own mouth that she has been betrayed by her lovers (Lam 1:19). But again, YHWH's words in her mouth are reaccented to evoke a different picture than the prophetic. In the prophet's account she is a painted as a temptress, a predator, whose deeds redound on her head. In her own account, she is a woman who, indeed, has taken lovers, but who is in distress because her lovers have betrayed her—not because she took them in the first place.[20] Remember that, in Hosea, the woman is (ostensibly) quoted as saying: "I will go after my lovers; they give me my bread and my water, my wool and my flax, my oil and my drink" (Hos 2:7). It was suggested before that this claim might indicate a lack in YHWH's provision and not necessarily support the traitorous tag that Hosea is trying to attach to her. Her candid admission of lovers in

---

20. I am not the only feminist reader who finds she can work against the text "not by resisting the text's description of the woman's function, but by following it stubbornly to the letter" (Sherwood 1996:265). To do otherwise, to my mind, is to collude in the text's ideology.

the context of despairing over their abandonment of her supports such a reading. It furthermore supports the contention that Zion's confession of sin should be read ironically, or at the very least that the "sin" of which she speaks may not be related to the alleged acts of adultery.

In addition to intertextual support, the rhetorical context of Lam 1:18a itself supports the contention that Zion is resisting the prophetic construction of her. In v. 18b, she says שִׁמְעוּ־נָא, ("listen well" or "listen up"), קָל־עַמִּים ("all peoples"), "and look upon my suffering." She is bringing a countersuit against YHWH, for which the people are called to be witnesses, which makes the idea of her having just admitted to rebellion seem somewhat untenable, or at least odd. She demands the people take account of her perspective as an alternative to the previous word spoken against her. Her point is that the enormity of her suffering works to mitigate her guilt: priests and elders have starved (1:19); warriors have been crushed (1:15); her children have gone into exile (1:5, 18); mothers are bereft (2:12); and her institutions have been obliterated (2:6–7). Daughter Zion may have been unfaithful, but how does that stack up against the wholesale slaughter of a people, a genocide to which God himself admits responsibility throughout prophetic texts? In Jer 5:26–29, YHWH implies that not all the people are deserving of punishment when he divides the populace into "scoundrels" and "others," but the vast majority of the remainder of the prophetic rhetoric makes it clear that he will punish indiscriminately "the nation," "the people," the "House of Jacob," "this city," "Jerusalem," "Daughter Zion."

If Zion had simply denied YHWH's accusation, and explicitly insisted on her innocence, we would be confronted with a hopeless "her word against His Word" (even if the latter is capital "H," capital "W"). Her resistance is far more radical than that: she is tearing at the very fabric of the retributive theology the prophets propound. Repentance articulated by the equation "I have sinned = You have no right to treat me this way" is clearly not what the prophets had in mind. It is epistemologically nonsensical in prophetic discourse (and often in ours).

Postcolonial theory is instructive here in its recognition that "colonial discourse typically rationalizes itself through rigid oppositions" (Gandhi: 32), in this case "sinner" versus "righteous." Like a colonial power, God does not paint in shades of grey. The cult-political status quo depends upon rigid moral categories. But the appalling enormity of her suffering forces the reevaluation of the justice of the retributive equation (based on strict binaries): sin/adultery = devastating punishment. What Leela Gandhi says of colonized subjects rings true for Zion: "The anti-colonial *'appropriator'* challenges the cultural and linguistic stability of the centre by *twisting old authoritarian words* into new oppositional meanings" (147). This is a form of "mimicry" and is a potent weapon in the anti-colonialist's arsenal. As L. Gandhi puts it, mimicry is the sly weapon of anti-colonial civility, an ambivalent mixture of deference and disobedience. The native subject often appears to observe the political and semantic imperatives of colonial discourse. But at the same time, she systematically misrepresents the foundational assumptions of this discourse. (150)

Such a reaccentuation of YHWH's allegation resonates with the ways colonized peoples (or women within patriarchy) have had to learn to negotiate the linguistic territory to which they are heirs. As Gandhi points out:

[T]he participants in an ethico-political dialogue are rarely equal, and almost never equally represented in the final consensus. Insofar as this dialogue is already projected towards some predetermined end—such as *justice* or rationality—it is always conducted . . . "within a field of possibilities that is already structured from the beginning in favour of certain outcomes." . . . The heterogeneity of thought . . . can only ever be preserved through the refusal of unanimity and the search for a radical "discensus." (28)

Zion works within the "field of possibilities," by which I mean we are not dealing with blasphemous speech here. She has not abandoned the religious discourse of her day. But within that field she reaches as far as possible toward "radical discensus" in the hopes of disrupting anticipated "outcomes," or as a hedge against foregone conclusions that might be oppressive to certain groups.

*Ezekiel and Zion's Indictment of YHWH*

A few passages from Ezek 16 and 23 suffice to round out this analysis. As J. Galambush and others have noted, there are several points of convergence between Ezekiel and Lam 1–2, especially Ezek 16:

The city's situation as described in Lamentations is remarkably like that *predicted* in Ezekiel. Those who "pass by" (2:15; Ezek 16:6, 8) are astonished that this city had once been called "perfect in beauty" (2:15; Ezek 16:14); she "remembers" her former complacency (1:7; Ezek 16:61, 63) after she has been punished for admitting foreigners to the sanctuary (1:10; Ezek 44:7 . . . ); she is compared unfavorably with Sodom (2:4; Ezek 16:48). . . . (58)

Chapter 16 begins with a long recitation describing YHWH's rescue of the orphan Jerusalem, daughter of a Hittite and Amorite. As it is not unusual for colonizers to keep subjects in place by feminizing them linguistically, so here Israel is the victim of YHWH's fantasy, the "exotic" foreign woman that he "rescues" from her barbaric origins. When he raises her to be his bride, she is expected to be grateful (Kanneh: 346). It should be noted that what YHWH raises his bride to be is a purely sexualized being; her attributes as a desirable woman are all that are emphasized. At this point, the rhetoric begins to echo that of Jeremiah's: YHWH decks her in fine jewels and linens, but she betrays him by making her beauty available to "any passerby"

(v. 15). In vv. 20–21, her sin of adultery is compounded with the crime of
infanticide (see also Ezek 23:37). The very children that YHWH and Zion
bore together, she slaughters and offers up to her lovers as a sacrifice. And
what is his punishment for this abominable act? In Lam 2:19 we read of the
destruction of Zion's children, "who faint for hunger at the head of every
street." The narrator beseeches Zion to cry for mercy to YHWH, the self-
proclaimed father of these children, for their lives. In Zion's own mouth
the parallelisms are even more powerful. In v. 20 she does cry out: "Look,
YHWH and consider! To whom (למי) have you done this?" Might the relative pronoun be referring to the children, his children, rather than to Zion
herself? For in the next line she asks rhetorically, "Should women eat their
own fruit, the children they have borne?" In Ezek 16:20, YHWH accuses her
of sacrificing their children; in Lamentations, the imagery of her (representing all mothers) eating their flesh seems in some sense an admission of
guilt, but in this case YHWH is the source behind such heinous acts. In short,
YHWH punishes the murder of his children by slaughtering them himself!
And the rhetoric of the second half of Lam 2:20 may be more vituperative
than suggested by the typical English translation. Although the Masoretic
pointing suggests that the root הרג be read as passive, "be slain," that it is a
singular verb suggests an active translation with YHWH as subject: "Should
YHWH slay . . . " (Kaiser: 179). In Lam 2:21, the use of the root טבח (tavachta)
indicates that Zion is throwing back into the face of YHWH the charge made
against her through the mouth of Ezekiel. As A. Berlin points out, the root
טבח is often used in the sense of "butchering meat in preparation for a
meal" (76). The children are being "sacrificed" by YHWH in order to serve at
the "festival day" that he has called (v. 22). My reading supports Berlin's
conclusion that the "God who slaughters his people is no less a cannibal
than the mothers who eat their children" (76). Like Job, Daughter Zion
here "closely imitates inherited speech, yet in ways that disclose some
hitherto unseen obscenity" (Newsom 2003:131). Her rhetoric in this case
takes a very similar form to the violence spewed by the prophetic texts, but
the obscenity it uncovers is YHWH's complicity in the slaughter of her/their
children. Moreover, in *Lamentations Rabbah*, the rabbis protest that YHWH's
crime is even worse than child sacrifice—He transgresses his own torah by
killing the mother with her "kid" (Lev 22:28).

At the end of this fiercely impassioned lament, Zion explicitly contradicts YHWH's construction of her and turns the prophetic rhetoric back
against her accuser when she states: "*Those whom I cherished/formed* (טפח)
*and reared* my enemy has consumed"[21] (from the root כלה—to finish, ex-
haust, consume) (v. 22). No ambiguity here about who "my enemy" is.
The assonance between טבח and טפח foregrounds for the hearers the contrast "you butchered," "I cherished/formed." The prophets and God enact

---

21. A. Berlin also prefers this translation.

a false construction of Zion's body. It is a body of lust and treachery, not a body that births and nurtures children; but by accusing him with imagery evocative of the sacrificial crimes of which he accused her, she has commuted the moral liability as construed in the prophetic texts and has wrested back some of her moral agency by transforming YHWH's sexualized and violent portrait of her into one that powerfully evokes bereft maternity, as well as common humanity.

Finally, beginning at Ezek 16:35, YHWH announces judgment against his errant wife (whom he calls "whore" [zonah]): "I will gather all your lovers.... I will gather them against you from all around, and will expose your genitals for them.... I will deliver you into their hands ... and they will gang rape you ... and stone you, and slice you in half with their swords" (16:37–40). First, child murder is punished with child murder, and here sexual infidelity is punished with rape (O'Connor 1999a:285).[22]

God/nations/husband, all use sexual violence to objectify and control Israel/wife and to legitimate their actions. Carole Sheffield explains that "in sexual terrorism ... two very important processes are at work ...: blaming the victim and absolving the offender. These tactics serve a vital political purpose: to protect our view of the world as orderly and just and to help us make sense of sexual violence" (69). Nelson makes a similar point with regard to the forces exerted to protect master narratives. The defenders of a given master narrative will commonly undermine the cognitive authority of its victims, usually either by dismissing counterclaims, citing a defect in the complainant's character, or by accusing "the victim of having provoked the harm" (161). But Zion will not collude in this falsehood. In Lam 1:10, the poet confirms Ezekiel's rape scenario with a less graphic version: "The enemy has stretched out his hand over all her precious things; she has even seen the nations come in to her sanctuary."[23] In this case, however, it is pointed out to YHWH that her violation means his as well. *Her* sanctuary is the House of YHWH. The end of v. 10 suggests that those he sent against her, those who invaded her sanctuary, are the very same ones to whom he had previously forbade entry when in Ezek 23:38–41, he chastises

---

22. Dobbs-Allsopp and Linafelt compare the curse section of the Sefire Treaty (IA, 40f.) with the rape imagery in Lamentations. From this evidence it seems possible to conclude that rape may indeed have been a punishment for a "loose woman" (80). And, of course, the discourse (not to mention the act!) of rape is a familiar one between colonizer and colonized (Kanneh: 347).

23. Dobbs-Allsopp and Linafelt show convincingly that this imagery is meant to evoke the metaphor of a woman raped. In addition, in a comparison with 2 Sam 13:20, they argue that *shomemah* (participle from שׁמם [to be desolated]) and *dawah* (adjective from דוה [faint]) in Lam 1:13 may "carry overtones of rape" (81). See also D. Guest (416, 419).

her for inviting "foreign" men into her sanctuary/the temple.[24] Their incursion results in the desecration of YHWH himself, but, paradoxically, YHWH sanctions their "entry" as a punishment against his wife for allowing their illicit entry. Lamentations thus reaccents the prophet's use of rape imagery to suggest that in endorsing the rape of his wife, YHWH has brought shame on both of them.[25] Such a paradox requires the reassessment of both the logic and justness of God's actions.

## Conclusion

Piece by piece, Daughter Zion constructs an alternative identity for herself by explaining her situation from her point of view. Lamentations 1–2 focuses on the two most damning pieces of evidence against Daughter Zion—that she has acted the "whore" and committed infanticide—and dismantles them by showing that they convey only partial truths. It is important to remember that a genuine commitment to dialogic reading means that we do not award the mantle of truth to, or unequivocally dismiss, any single discourse: Both God and Zion inevitably have portions of the truth to tell about their relationship. But this chapter takes what I see as an important first step in reading dialogically by temporarily privileging a voice that traditionally has been suppressed. Even if most readers privilege YHWH's version of events, the biblical writers, editors, and compilers saw fit to include Daughter Zion's account. Likewise, while YHWH's speech is often monologic, the canon is not. As a result, while YHWH may not always garner my respect, the biblical text unfailingly does because it is dialogically constituted, through and through. As such, we should let biblical form serve as a model for our reading practices.

Because midrash is one of the most intrinsically dialogic hermeneutic systems that has been developed, I conclude with a rabbinic midrash that captures the spirit of my reading of Daughter Zion. In the famous passage in Jer 31:15–17 of Rachel weeping for her children,[26] God responds to

---

24. See J. Galambush for an explanation of these verses in Ezekiel as referring to illicit temple intrusion by Jerusalem's foreign allies (81).

25. As J. Galambush notes, "The [marriage] metaphor demands Yahweh's vulnerability" (53), although she also stresses that, in Ezekiel, YHWH maintains his control through his "gaze" and his control of other men's gazes. Dennis Tucker's recent claim that the relationship between supplicant and YHWH in the lament psalms is one based on honor and shame within the parameters of a patron-client configuration might explain to some extent Daughter Zion's rhetorical goals here. She is pointing out that in not upholding his duties as patron, YHWH is shaming both himself and his "wife."

26. In Lamentations, we hear Rachel weeping, too, but outside of the prophetic discourse God's silence highlights the truth about her condition—there is no facile hope; dead children don't come back (regardless of what Isa 49 and 54 would like us to believe).

her weeping with words of comfort. Perceptively, in *Lamentations Rabbah* (Petihta 24), the rabbis give Rachel a subjectivity the biblical story does not as Rachel takes God to task for her children. She does not understand that if she, a mere woman, could be generous enough to put aside her jealousy and share her beloved with her sister, the master of the universe cannot do as much: "[W]hy should you, everlasting and merciful king, be jealous of idolatry in which there is no reality." In the rabbis' version, God, thus confronted, answers and acquiesces in his punishment (Laytner: 127). In Lamentations, of course, he does no such thing, but one would suppose that the fire in Daughter Zion's discourse struck the rabbis as unique among biblical speech directed toward God, and inspired this fable. In the rabbinic tale, Rachel does not respond, but as we know from Jeremiah, Rachel refuses to be comforted—dead children cannot come home.[27] Likewise, in Second Isaiah we see Daughter Zion refuse to be comforted for the loss of her children.

---

27. Neusner's translation of *Lamentations Rabbah* (1989:78–79).

# 5

# God "Speaks Tenderly" to Jerusalem?

*A voice is heard in Ramah, lamentation and bitter weeping. Rachel is weeping for her children; she refuses to be comforted for her children who are no more.* (Jer 31:15)

God's silence in Lamentations leaves us "with an unresolved tension between the silence of God and epic human suffering"; in other words, it evokes the age-old question of theodicy, a question to which a response is required (Turner: 197). Second Isaiah is that response,[1] but is it adequate? Lamentations 2 ends with Zion's unmitigated rage. Is it a discourse to which *any* response could be adequate? O'Connor posits that "because God never speaks, the book honors voices of pain" (2002:15; 85). If this is so, then when God finally does speak in Second Isaiah, the onus is on him to speak in a way that honors pain in the same way his silence did.

We noted previously that Zion's complaint makes almost no specific request of YHWH. Unlike Job she does not even demand a response. Rather, self-expression seems to be both the function and *telos* of her discourse. The only explicit request she makes comes at the end of Lam 1, when it seems the injustice of her situation gets the best of her and she pleads with YHWH to wreak the same punishment on her enemies that she had to endure. If she is guilty then surely they, who have decimated her, are equally answerable. Her vengeful speech seems somewhat out of place in a discourse that has otherwise been focused on her experiences. And in fact, it is her last such request. Although her primary need has been to voice her grief, YHWH feels moved—probably for his own reasons, as we will see—to respond to her grievance, as well as to some of her more

---

1. "From Daughter Zion's intertextual history, Second Isaiah crafts his poems. He uses her story, replies to it, and expands it, alluding to her history linguistically, thematically, and narratively" (O'Connor 1999a:287). O'Connor charts all the places where Second Isaiah responds to Lamentations fairly directly (290–91).

implicit requests. He attempts to woo her back, although reconciliation is not something she explicitly requests. Still, that YHWH makes the effort to woo her at all demonstrates the importance the Bible and its deity attach to dialogic relationships, even if God does not always go about securing them in the most effective ways. Second Isaiah's (I limit this designation to Isa 40–55) intense dialogic interaction with several biblical texts has long been recognized, but with no other biblical text does its response intone as dramatically as with Lamentations.[2]

> Initially in Lamentations, Daughter Zion accepts blame for her predicament (1:18), as she did in Jer 4:19–20, 31, but quickly she shifts the focus to divine culpability. . . . God never sees, never comforts, never replies to Zion's accusations that his anger is out of control, that he destroys without mercy (2:2). How dramatic then are Second Isaiah's opening words where YHWH responds directly to the conditions of Daughter Zion in Lamentations. (O'Connor 1999a:286)

Second Isaiah and Lamentations share terms that describe Zion and her condition. She "sighs," is "swallowed up," "afflicted," and so on,[3] but in Second Isaiah these qualifiers are reversed or inverted (Turner: 200).[4] As P. Tull Willey points out, it seems clear that Second Isaiah quite deliberately borrowed from and reworked previous texts and traditions to fit an altered situation (1995:275).

Isaiah 40, for example, begins God's response to Lamentations with an echo of a refrain that runs throughout Lam 1–2: "Comfort (נחם), comfort my people." Five times in Lamentations we are told that Zion has no one to comfort her. General comparisons between Lamentations and Second Isaiah as well as comparisons between the Servant and Zion songs within Second Isaiah have been well covered in the past two decades, with much of the effort going to make up for the way the Zion songs have been overshadowed by the attention given to the Servant songs.[5] I will not, therefore, traverse the same territory except where it is crucial to my thesis. I will,

---

2. Sawyer and Tull Willey have helped me see that some echoes between Lamentations and Second Isaiah are accounted for because both are referring to the Book of Jeremiah. But canonically speaking, there is no priority—intertextually they are all chatting.

3. Turner provides a more exhaustive list of the vocabulary shared and the verses.

4. Using Laurent Jenny, Tull Willey discusses a variety of ways in which a later author recapitulates an earlier text (1996:76). One of those ways is called "inversion": "changes that can be quite varied, and may involve a change in the speaker or the addressee; a change in the modifiers so as to be characterized antithetically; a reversal of the dramatic situation by negative or passive transformation; or a reversal of symbolic values."

5. See, for example, M. E. Biddle; P. Tull Willey 1995, 1997; K. O'Connor 1999a; and J. F. A. Sawyer.

instead, continue to keep my focus on the "conversation" between YHWH and Zion. I am interested primarily in the particulars of God's discourse in Second Isaiah as it functions as a response to Lam 1–2—primarily Isa 49, 51, 52, 54. In general, I want to know if Second Isaiah's "story" is more in accord with Zion's self-story or with YHWH's story about her in Jeremiah and Ezekiel. This will allow me to gauge how well he has heard her, and to what extent he seeks genuine reconciliation. I focus therefore on second-person feminine singular speech and on interrogating the text with the following questions: What issues raised by Zion does YHWH choose to address? From which angle does he approach the issue? To what does he neglect to respond? What seems to be the ultimate agenda of his response? How do his words differ from previous prophetically mediated words? What theological insights does his response make available to us? And ultimately, "Can the one who is the perpetrator of violence against Daughter Zion also be the one who redeems her from it?" (Turner: 200–201). Many exegetes have answered an unequivocal "yes" to this last question. Buying into the explicit story line put forward in the text, John Sawyer says, for example, "Through these chapters [Isa 49–66], in a series of dramatic poems, runs the story of a woman's life from bereavement and barrenness in chapter 49 to the birth of a son in chapter 66" (91). What Sawyer does not ask is whether a birth can undo the deaths of previous children.

Before moving on to the Isaianic texts that directly address Zion, let's start with the only speech of Zion in Lamentations that qualifies as an explicit request. In Lam 1:22 she beseeches God: "Let all their wrongdoing come before you, and deal with them as you have dealt with me." Zion does not ask for a reprieve, only justice through vengeance. In addition to the straightforward desire for revenge, Zion's request might also hint at a deep-seated sense of anxiety. Given the theological, political, and ideological consequences of a god who fails to protect his people, it is not surprising to hear the poet of Lamentations try to rouse God to vanquish Zion's (and God's) enemies. Divine impotence is a concern that haunts much prophetic (and Deuteronomic-influenced) discourse—Jeremiah and Ezekiel are quick to fault humanity for their own downfall and stress that Judah's enemies are prevailing only by divine sanction. Even Second Isaiah, a prophet who to a degree is willing to explore the deity's faults, does not come near to implying that YHWH is lacking in muscle. YHWH may have erred in using too much force, but the attribution of weakness is unthinkable. In any case, whether or not she is harboring any doubts in this regard, Zion requests that YHWH show himself capable of routing her enemies. As if in response, much of Second Isaiah's rhetoric seems addressed to this plea. It makes sense that YHWH's discourse focuses on the one explicit request Zion makes because it is one of her few utterances that shift the blame away from YHWH. With talk of vanquishing enemies, God is in his comfort zone. Early on the prophet is concerned to demonstrate YHWH's prowess against his enemies: "The nations are but a drop in the bucket, reckoned as dust on a balance; the very coastlands he lifts like motes" (Isa 40:15). Mark Biddle makes this one of the primary points of a recent article. He focuses on the downfall of "Lady Babylon" in Isa 47 as a reversal of the violent supremacy she exercised against Lady Zion. Reminiscent of the personification of Zion, Babylon is addressed directly as "Daughter Babylon" or "Daughter Chaldea" (Isa 47:1a, 1b, 4). The violence she has perpetrated against Zion will redound upon her, she will be stripped naked and shamed (47:3)—familiar language from Jeremiah and Ezekiel. Ironically, YHWH admits that it was his anger that unleashed Babylon's fury against Zion (47:6), but in the end he passes the buck to Babylon: "I gave them into your hands; you did not show them mercy. On the old ones you made your yoke exceedingly heavy" (47:6b–c). YHWH shows little in the way of awareness of his own excesses, even though as the prophet himself proclaimed at the beginning of his revelation: "For [Jerusalem] has received at the hand of YHWH *double* for all her sins" (Isa 40:2). And in Lam 1:19 and 2:10, the "old ones" are referred to specifically as suffering YHWH's wrath. But if his mercy was previously absent, the whole point of his present discourse is to activate that once latent mercy. Irony and semantic slippage characterize YHWH's speech in Second Isaiah, because the poet is walking a tightrope between the binaries of YHWH's power/impotence and his mercy/justice. If YHWH is indeed in control of Judah's destiny then he is responsible for her destruction, but if he is responsible then how to make sense of Babylon's guilt? Whether logical or not, the rhetoric is what the disheartened exiles would want to hear—YHWH is in control, and Judah's enemies are going to feel his wrath.

In a fashion similar to Jeremiah's occasional quotations of Zion, Daughter Babylon's thoughts are reported as echoing two major themes of Zion's downfall in Lamentations: "I shall not become a *widow* or know the loss of *children*" (Isa 48:8). YHWH counters her self-assurance by assuring her that, to the contrary, "These two things will come upon you suddenly, in one day: Loss of children and widowhood will come upon you in full measure" (Isa 48:9). Lamentations 1–2 of course focuses on these very themes, as they emotionally figure Zion's ruin. The gendered rendering of these two cities is not incidental to the message of the text. The cities' experiences as a whole will closely resemble a woman who is made bereft of her children, and who is left unprotected by male kin. The effects of sin and powerlessness will dominate their emotional horizon. Notably, the language used by YHWH in Isa 47 lacks the vehemence and vulgarity that characterize similar proclamations against Zion in the earlier prophets. An absence of the intimacy that marks the metaphor of marriage may account for the decrease in fiery language. Zion met her fate because she was disloyal to her god/husband. Babylon will meet her fate because of loyalty to the wrong powers—YHWH claims that Babylon's commitment to her cult of magic and astrology has betrayed her (Isa 40:9–13). This is congruent with Second Isaiah's attack on the pseudo-gods of Babylon (Isa 44:9–17), a tactic used by the prophet as part of his campaign to urge the exiles to support Persia and to ignite their passion to return and rebuild Judah as a bastion of unwavering YHWHism (Isa 44:24–28; 45:1–4). All in all, Isa 47 functions as a satisfying answer to Zion's request that her enemies be treated as she has been: Babylon is feminized, subject to rape and humiliation, widowed and bereaved of her children. Furthermore, it is implied that Daughter Chaldea is punished for following the "wrong" gods, a charge made explicit in Zion's case, as well. This retributive flurry constitutes a too easy response for YHWH—the promise to flex his muscles.[6] It costs him nothing and ultimately sidesteps the real issue for Daughter Zion—his culpability for her torment. The anti-Babylon rhetoric reflects the conflicted colonial status of this text. It is at the same time a colonial and postcolonial document, although colonial forces overall have the strongest impact. Babylon's imperial conquests brought down Judah, and Second Isaiah can be read as resisting the colonizing forces to which it previously succumbed and as an attempt by the exiles to hold on to their customs in a foreign land. On the other hand, many scholars have noted the pro-Persian slant of these chapters (Berquist: 22–23). The designation of "messiah" bestowed on the Persian monarch, Darius (Isa 45), is one obvious example. Second Isaiah is a document trapped between two urgent but potentially mutually exclusive needs—the survival of an authentic indigenous identity and survival, period—a situation not unlike Daughter Zion's as reflected in earlier prophetic texts.[7]

Except for a smattering of references to a feminized Jerusalem, much of the first half of Second Isaiah is addressed to or references the "servant," or a second-person masculine singular addressee most assume is the servant. It is not until Isa 49 that Zion makes her first speaking appearance. As was the case in Jeremiah, Zion's speech is only reported in indirect discourse by the prophet/deity. In this case, however, the introduction of the quote by the simple formulation ותאמר ציון ("And Zion says"), without any other kind of set-up, makes her words seem less mediated, almost as if they were lifted from a text such as Lamentations, in which her words convey directly. We might even read the introduction as referencing a past text: as in "Zion said." What she says (or said) is strikingly incongruous with the verse upon verse, chapter upon chapter of oracles of salvation that lead up to this brief speech: "YHWH has forsaken me; my lord has abandoned me" (49:14). Immediately preceding this dismal proclamation, YHWH responds to a speech by the servant, saying:

---

6. Mary Donovan Turner says that God's words of comfort in Second Isaiah are words that "come too easily" (203).

7. Norman Gottwald offers a sociological explanation of the competing demands for identity maintenance versus political expediency. The situation is further complicated by the fact that Second Isaiah's audience was surely the former political elite of Judah, a colonizing group in their own right.

> Thus says YHWH:
> In an hour of favor I answer you,
> and on a day of salvation I help you.
> I created you and appointed you a covenant people—
> restoring the land,
> allotting anew the desolate holdings,
> saying to the prisoners, "Go free,"
> to those in darkness, "Show yourselves." (Isa 49:8–9)

The speech ends with the hymnic refrain:

> Shout, heavens, and rejoice, earth!
> Break into shouting, hills!
> For YHWH has *comforted* his people,
> and has had compassion on his afflicted ones. (Isa 49:13)

Directly on the heels of such jubilation, Zion's words—"YHWH has forsaken me"—strike a discordant note.

> The claim of YHWH's abandonment . . . in the mouth of Daughter Zion in Second Isaiah . . . occurs not only long after the opening announcement of Zion's consolation, but after eight chapters of nearly continuous divine speech. Heaven, earth, and mountains have been invited to rejoice at the news of YHWH's redemption. This cosmic celebration is halted by Zion's words. (Tull Willey 1995:281)

Unmoved by YHWH's declarations, Zion apparently remains just as un-comforted as we left her in Lamentations (O'Connor 2002:13). Perhaps her speech is meant to precipitate a separate divine declaration, directed toward her, similar to the Servant's speech at the start of the chapter that precipitated the divine declaration that ends at v. 13. One cannot help being struck, however, by the difference in tone between the Servant's speech (49:1–6)—which is also much lengthier—and Zion's speech. The Servant's speech has a similarly brief exclamation of despair (v. 4), but it comes in the context of a discourse of trust and an already answered plea. In comparison, Zion's brief remark comes across as pathetic, in every sense. Undeterred by her despondency, YHWH's response is considered. Appealing to her feminine sensibilities and sympathies, YHWH figures him-self as a woman; he could no more forget her than a mother could forget her own child. And even if she could forget, his love is surpassing (49:15). His metaphor may fall on deaf ears, however, since Zion, as reported in Lamentations, has seen mothers "forget" to the point of cannibalizing their own children, but YHWH appears unaware of the irony. While mothers may have been forced to do heinous things, ultimately Daughter Zion's great-est grief comes from the children she has lost—and YHWH's next statement takes account of this: not only does he put a maternal face on divinity, he assures her, "Swiftly your children are coming. . . . Lift up your eyes and look all around, they are gathered and coming to you" (49:18). Charac-teristic of the exuberance of this prophecy, she is told that soon she will have so many children that her land will be cramped with them. Also done away with is any sense that YHWH should be likened to her enemies. YHWH declares that her destroyers—clearly not alluding to himself—will stay at a remove (49:19; see also Isa 51:13; cf. Lam 2:4). As if waking from a dream, Zion will learn that she was mistaken in thinking her children lost (49:20). Bewildered, she will ask where these children came from, surely not from her since she was "bereaved and barren, exiled and disdained" (49:21b). This hypothetical presentation of her state of mind coming from YHWH's mouth is meant to signify the mystery and awesomeness of what YHWH is about to do, but read from Zion's point of view—keeping in mind her own presentation in Lam 1–2—it can be read more plainly as doubt about the possibility of children rising from the dead: "I was left all alone; these, where were they?" (49:21c). Furthermore, peering behind the text, we know that the return of these "children" may not have occasioned rejoicing for those that remained in the land of Judah these several decades. The children who are being urged to return to Judah might better be considered colonists than Zion's beloved returning (Berquist: 32). This highlights what is otherwise canonically hidden—that Second Isaiah's rhetoric specifically privileges the *golah* community; it does not speak to the suffering of those left in Judah, the probable creators of Lamentations. Their children are not coming home—Zion's children are irrevocably lost.

In apparent acknowledgment that Zion will be a harder sell on this point, YHWH presses the issue, "Can captives be retrieved from a victor?" (49:24). He answers himself, "Captives will be taken from a warrior . . . and I will deliver your children!" (49:25). Furthermore, the kings and queens of the "nations" shall care for her children and will lick the dust of her feet in obeisance (49:23). In a gruesomely insensitive response to the cannibalistic horrors she was forced to witness (Lam 2:20), YHWH proclaims that her "oppressors will eat their own flesh and be drunk with their own blood"—all this so she might come to know that YHWH is indeed her savior and redeemer (49:26). That she should come to such knowledge seems against all odds at this point, and the overweening zeal of Second Isaiah's rhetoric reflects the uphill battle in which he is engaged.[8] A new oracle begins at chapter 50 that temporarily switches addressee to Zion's children. Still rebutting the evidence of her experience, YHWH now asks Zion's children to believe that he never divorced their mother, nor do the creditors to whom he sold them off exist anymore (50:1a). Again, however, there is slippage—he did sell them off and did dismiss their mother (50:1b); but this time he claims it was for *their* crimes, not hers.[9] Verse 2, if semantically

---

8. Isaiah 50:4 may be an allusion to the prophet's difficult task of speaking to those who are so "beat up" it takes special rhetorical skill to rouse them.

9. "Like Jer 3:13, this verse goes on to identify the problem as sins and transgressions. Though Jeremiah attributes these to the wife, Second Isaiah blames the children" (Tull Willey 1995:284). This is quite a different tack than that taken in

connected to the preceding verse, demonstrates some disingenuousness on YHWH's part: "On account of what was no one there when I came; and no one responded when I called?" is reminiscent of YHWH's calling Adam and Eve in the garden after they have eaten of the apple, or his question to Cain after he has slain his brother. In Genesis the rhetorical questions are calling attention to human sin. These questions, if I am reading them right, are also meant as a slap on the wrist to those who do not have faith in YHWH's saving power. The questions this time, however, cannot help but draw attention to YHWH's misdeeds: Where are they and why haven't they answered? They are in exile, that's where; and struck dumb by the hand of their god, that's why. Still, it seems a rhetorically effective way of instigating the desired response from the people: "If our god takes this expectation for granted, then everything must be okay!" In other words, if the divorce never happened and their servitude is no longer a reality, then what is holding them back from reuniting with God? Surely for some, such a message sounded a liberating note, while others certainly would have trouble trusting again. On which side would Zion, as a speaker-actor in this drama, find herself? The degree of utter hopelessness expressed in Lam 1–2 and the sole instance of her speech in Second Isaiah (49:14) suggests she falls in the latter category. The contrast with the Servant in this regard is marked: "The lord YHWH opened my ears, and I did not disobey, I did not run away" (50:5). Unfortunately, with regard to the gendered implications, Zion's positive response is not genuinely elicited or desired. The ultimate goal is to rouse the "children" to return to their "mother," and the representation of the Servant merges with that of the children, while Zion is largely an outsider in the rhetoric of reconciliation.[10]

It is not until 51:17 that we have another sustained speech that is addressed to the woman. This section resonates strongly with Lamentations language. Even the style of the speech is reminiscent of the (DV) speaker in Lam 1–2. In a formal similarity to Lam 1–2, it alternates between speech directed to and speech about Zion. Immediately prior to this speech (51:12–16), YHWH addresses a mixed masculine singular and masculine plural audience. The section finishes with a transition to the Zion speech: "I have said to Zion: You [m.s.] are my people!" (51:16). As the speech shifts to a feminine singular audience, the identity of the speaker shifts as well.

the previous prophetic accusations. One possibility is that even as he turns his speech on the children, the rhetoric is meant for Zion, as a means of lightening her load and wooing her back.

10. D. Rom-Shiloni has made an intriguing discovery that has some bearing on this observation. In her study of political and familial metaphors in Ezekiel, she notes that the prophecies employing metaphors that figure the divine-human relationship in terms of a sovereign and his people tend to end hopefully (Ezek 20), while those prophecies that employ the marriage metaphor end in utter annihilation (Ezek 16) (Society of Biblical Literature Annual Meeting, 2006).

No longer is YHWH doing the talking, but the prophet. Initially, the speaker urges Jerusalem to "rouse herself" and "arise." This plea calls to mind the narrator's plea in Lam 2:19: "Arise, cry out in the night!" which clearly has negative connotations. She is to cry out from the midst of ongoing misfortune. In the Isaianic context, one gets the sense that the call to "arise" forecasts an improved situation. But the nature of the improvement is not immediately broadcast. From what she should rouse herself and arise becomes apparent as the next several verses detail the horror of her treatment at YHWH's hand.

> You who from YHWH's hand
> Have drunk the cup of his wrath,
> You who have drained to the dregs
> The bowl, the cup of reeling. (Isa 51:17)

This statement comes close to an admission of guilt but does not achieve its dialogic potential, because YHWH is not the speaker. Except that it is not addressed to Zion directly, Lam 2 opens with similar imagery.

> The Lord in his wrath
> Has shamed Daughter Zion;
> . . .
> He did not remember his footstool
> On the day of his wrath. (Lam 2:1)

The prophet then switches into third-person feminine singular speech that again echoes thematically much of what we heard in the poet's speech of Lam 1–2.

> She has none to guide her
> Of all the sons she bore;
> None takes her by the hand,
> Of all the sons she reared. (Isa 51:18)

> My eyes are spent with tears,
> My heart is in tumult,
> My innards are in turmoil
> Over the ruin of the daughter of my people,
> As babes and sucklings languish
> In the squares of the city. (Lam 2:11)

These quotes are thematically similar. Second Isaiah and the narrator/DV of Lam 1–2 constitute a genuinely empathetic response to Zion's pain. God's response, on the other hand, falls short because he cannot quite admit what they do—that he acted out of all proportion. Having said that, Second Isaiah's goals are different from the expressive and emotive goals of the speakers of Lam 1–2. His is persuasive rhetoric, meant to win over hearts and minds. Each speech unit is thus geared toward convincing a particular audience to trust and return to YHWH. As such the rhetoric is of the type, "I acknowledge that you have suffered in these ways, but be as-

sured that God is about to relieve your suffering." Only the first half of this
equation is represented in Lam 1–2.

The next two verses in Isa 51 also recall both vocabulary and themes
from Lam 1–2.

> These two things have befallen you:
> Wrack and ruin—who can console you?
> Famine and sword—who will/how will I comfort you?
> Your sons lie in a swoon
> At the corner of every street,
> Like an antelope caught in a net,
> Drunk with the wrath of YHWH,
> With the rebuke of your god. (Isa 51:19–20)

It seems plausible that Lam 2:13 served as the impetus for the prophet's
words.

> To what can I compare or liken you,
> Daughter Jerusalem?
> To what can I match you to comfort you,
> Maiden Daughter Zion?
> For vast as the sea is your ruin;
> Who can heal you?

Both pick up the theme of her incomparable suffering, although they use
different metaphors—an animal caught in a net (see Lam 1:13) and the
vastness of the sea—for emphasis. Both address her directly and with
great compassion and emotive force. Both use the root שבר to describe her
"ruin," and, most telling, both stress the incomparability of her situation
by asking a rhetorical question: How can she be comforted (נחם)? Even
more telling is the grammatical mistake made by the prophet in forming
the question. It is clear that in Isa 51:19, in which the prophet should say
"who will comfort you," he is directly borrowing from Lam 2:13 with its
first-person form because the prophet says instead "who, I will comfort
you?" picking up on the form used in Lam 2:13 (נחמך). After the long interlude that follows the initial call to "arise!" the prophet finally gets around
to delivering the oracle of salvation.

> Thus says your lord, YHWH,
> Your God who champions his people:
> Herewith I take from your hand
> the cup of reeling,
> The bowl, the cup of my wrath;
> You shall never drink it again. (Isa 51:22)

He will put the cup of his wrath, instead, into the hands of Zion's enemies
(Isa 51:23), as she requested in Lam 1:21–22.

One might expect some response on Zion's part. In Lamentations, her
voice mixes with the poet-narrator's, and she even seems at times to be

responding to his prompts, as at the end of Lam 2. There is no response, however, leaving the reader without a sense of closure with regard to the spousal relationship. YHWH's salvation is proclaimed, but there is no hymn of praise or thanksgiving from the one apparently being redeemed. If the Book of Psalms can serve as a comparison, we should expect some kind of thanksgiving in response to an answered supplication. Hannah's prayers in 1 Sam 1:9–2:10 are an example of this process embedded in narrative. But this section in Second Isaiah simply peters out . . .

> I will put it in the hands of your tormentors,
> Who have commanded you,
> "Get down, that we may walk over you,"
> so that you made your back like the ground,
> Like a street for passersby. (Isa 51:23)

It is an oddly dismal note on which to end in this context. To his credit, the prophet-poet seems to put his heart and soul into the project of offering Zion compassion and hope and seems to do a better job of acknowledging her point of view than YHWH does. He does not sugarcoat YHWH's harsh treatment of her, nor the intensity of her suffering. All said, he fully acknowledges the justness of her complaint. So, her silence is troubling. The reconciliation that seems to have been achieved between the Servant and God is lacking for Zion and God. Is there some suffering that is simply impassable? There is a suffering that reduces one to silence in which "the person no longer has a sense of personal agency" (Turner: 201) and for which language fails. Previously, however, extreme suffering led to an outpouring of emotion by Zion. Something else seems to be at work here. I discussed at length in chapter 3 how Zion's speech in Lam 1–2 denotes a reclamation of her agency, but in Second Isaiah, as in the earlier prophetic texts, there seems to be no room for her speech. Even with Second Isaiah's stabs at empathy, when all is said and done, this is prophetic space, divine space, DV space, the "Father's" space, logocentric space. Monologism reigns. Tull Willey makes this point in her discussion of Bakhtin and Second Isaiah.

> The novels that Bakhtin portrayed as dialogical novels *par excellence*, those of Dostoevsky, reflected competing voices without resolving whose voice should be taken as authoritative. In that sense they are very different from second Isaiah which, though shot through with dialogue, allows one voice to dominate over all others from beginning . . . to end. . . . Only YHWH and YHWH's herald, who speaks so much in concert with YHWH that they are at times difficult to distinguish, are authorized to interpret the coming events. In this way Second Isaiah . . . enacts the silencing of any voice but its own. (1997:75–76)

The bottom line is that Jeremiah and Second Isaiah, while contradicting each other in many particulars, are both in the business of defending YHWH's privilege; only Lam 1–2 provides a genuinely alternate point of view, specifically the victim's point of view. Beyond the fact that prophetic space is not open to Zion (but also consequent to that fact), another way of looking at Zion's silence is from her perspective. She is not going to make amends easily. She may be viewed as refusing to take part in a discursive event that still refuses to engage authentically her point of view. In contrast, the Servant is given a legitimate place in the text's rhetoric. The Servant longs for God and, unlike Zion, seems comfortable talking to God and making requests. This comparison is paralleled in Lamentations, whereby Zion's utter estrangement in Lam 1–2 is contrasted to Lam 3, where the masculine singular speaker, while still lamenting, seems much more in step with typical prophetic theology. If we were to drop Zion's speech from Lam 1–2 into Deutero-Isaiah, it would represent a subversive force that could undermine the prophet's goals. Thus she is spoken about, spoken to, and alluded to, but not allowed a voice of her own, except once. Interestingly, given its brevity, her voice packs a pretty subversive wallop, but only when read in view of Zion's previous speech in Lamentations, and with a dialogic awareness of the power dynamics at work between the prophetic texts and Lam 1–2.

Although Isa 51:17–23 seems to trail off, the energy picks back up in the next section addressed to Zion, as if the prophet is trying again. I am inclined to think that 52:1–2 forms a semantic unit with the previous Zion section, which, as I noted, lacks closure on its own. Isaiah 52:1–2 is a small section, but it covers some themes from Lam 1–2 neglected by the previous section. The previous segment began by rallying the woman to "rouse yourself" and "arise." Chapter 52 begins with the same root, עור ("awake"), but different form, repeated twice, as in 51:17: "Awake, awake, Zion! Clothe yourself in splendor." The feminine singular address continues: "Put on your robes of majesty, Jerusalem, holy city; for the uncircumcised and the unclean will never enter you again." The proclamation of the city's holiness reverses the description of her uncleanness in Lam 1:9, while the promise that the unclean will never again enter her recalls and overturns Lam 1:10, in which the metaphor of rape is used to describe the invasion of the temple by the unclean nations. In both cases, the verb בוא is used to describe the illicit penetration. The command to clothe herself in robes of majesty undoes the harsh imagery of stripping that was disturbingly common in the previous prophetic texts (e.g., Hos. 2:5; Jer 13:26; Ezek 16:37; etc.). The short section ends with more imperatives: "Shake off the dust; arise, sit [on your throne?], Jerusalem! Loose the bonds from your neck, captive Daughter Zion!" Lamentations 1–2 has several allusions to Zion's "fallen" state that Isa 52:1–2 reverses: YHWH has "cast down" her majesty (2:1), "her elders sit on the ground with dust on their head" (2:10), she who was once a "princess" is become a thrall (1:1), and YHWH's yoke weighs heavy on her (1:14). All that is in the past. Her salvation is announced; the time has come to rise from the dust, to reassume a position of honor, to no longer be bound like a servant. The voice of the speaker of this section is ambiguous, but with regard to style, tone, and content, it appears to be the continuation of the previous speaker's voice. There is nothing to suggest conclusively that it is YHWH's voice. At 52:3, YHWH's voice steps in, but he addresses himself to a masculine plural audience. YHWH and the woman have engaged in very little dialogue to this point. This is partly the effect of her nearly absolute silence, but, additionally, the deity addresses her very rarely outside of chapter 49. The only other time in chapter 52 that the woman is addressed it is by a herald announcing to her, "Your god is king" (v. 7).

The culmination of the redeeming speech directed toward Zion comes nearly at the end of Second Isaiah, at least insofar as the traditional division between Second and Third Isaiah stands. In chapter 54 the rhetoric of salvation meant to court Zion reaches a crescendo. She is addressed directly throughout, ostensibly by YHWH himself, although there is some voicing ambiguity typical of prophetic communication. There is little in this chapter that suggests a direct dependence on Lam 1–2, although it addresses several of the concerns voiced there in a general way. Many of the themes chapter 54 shares with Lam 1–2—loss of children, widowhood, YHWH's anger, marriage metaphor, and so on—are common as well to the earlier prophetic texts, especially Jeremiah, and so may equally be serving as a response to some of those texts. Because the connections between chapter 54 and Jeremiah have been explored in other studies, and because it would not serve the specific goals of this study to chart those connections, I focus on aspects of chapter 54 that seem to address Zion's concerns in Lam 1–2, whether intentional or not.

The first part of the chapter is concerned with the return of the exiles. Zion's children will return to her in such abundance that the land will hardly contain them (54:1–3). There is no mention of their suffering. In the second unit, vv. 4–6, YHWH attends to the issues of shame and espousal that were explicit in the previous prophets and that served as part of Lam 1–2's gestalt. He urges her to trust that the time of her shame and disgrace is over. Apparently related to the theme of shamefulness is his promise to reverse her widowhood; speaking of himself in the third person, YHWH vows that "YHWH of hosts," the "god of all the earth," will "espouse" her and thereby "redeem" her (reminiscent of his initial betrothal in Ezekiel). The section ends with a rhetorical question: "Can one cast off the wife of his youth?" (54:6c). This rhetorical tactic is consonant with previous verses that made everything that happened to Zion in the past seem like some kind of dream, or otherwise unreality. While it is meant purely rhetorically, one cannot help but imagine the addressees scratching their heads and giving the question some serious contemplation. Either one can indeed cast off the wife of his youth, or the fall of Jerusalem with its subsequent horrors was an aberration of cosmic proportions. The prophet seems to be urging them to understand their experience as something so bizarre that it should no longer be called to mind, nor its return feared. YHWH makes a vow to this effect in the next section. After admitting to his temporary anger, he pledges everlasting faithfulness and compassion (54:8), even comparing the horror and promise of the situation to the mythic terror of the flood: "For this is to me like the waters [or "days"] of Noah; as I swore that the waters of Noah nevermore would flood the earth, so I swear that I will not be angry with you or rebuke you" (54:9). And then comes a refrain that rhetorically echoes the opening of the chapter: "Unhappy and storm-tossed one, not comforted! I will lay carbuncles[11] as your building stones and make your foundation of sapphires!" (54:11). It begins with an acknowledgment of her unfortunate situation, then moves into language that reverses the negative designation.[12] It is interesting that after all the attempts to "comfort" Zion (49:13) thus far—as well as the claim that YHWH is her "comforter" (51:12)—that here she is referred to as "not comforted." It is the instance of YHWH's speech that most directly acknowledges her situation as expressed in Lam 1–2. Taking responsibility for her suffering makes his promises seem more believable. J. Sawyer says that in 54:1–10 YHWH "takes prime responsibility for the tragedy and swears he will never again be angry with her or rebuke her" (94). K. O'Connor also sees virtue in YHWH's owning up to this indiscrete use of violence (1999a:292). In Isa 54:7–8, "[H]e abandoned her, in his fury he hid from her, not the other way around. Her interpretation of their separation in Lamentations was completely accurate. Now he promises his *hesed* will be as permanent as his covenant with Noah." Still, with the recognition of her comfortless state, his promises may be too facile—her edifices will be rebuilt with precious gems, her children will be happy, she will be safe from oppression and ruin. Perhaps when all these things actually come to pass, Zion can respond accordingly. J. Sawyer makes a comment that bears on this:

> Yahweh, "the Holy One of Israel . . . God of all the earth" (v. 5), is represented as behaving like a remorseful husband, pleading with his wife to trust him and take him back . . . He has the power to give her happiness and dignity and freedom; she knows he also has the power to punish, humiliate and abuse her. So he has to convince her that he really loves her and that she can trust him. (95–96)

---

11. Following the JPS translation.

12. The City Laments of Mesopotamia have resonances with Second Isaiah. Dobbs-Allsopp notes in fact that the City Laments more closely resemble Second Isaiah in their comic trajectory (2002:11). One example specific to this section's discussion of rebuilding the destroyed city appears in "The Lamentation Over the Destruction of Sumer and Ur," in which, in lines 341–42, one god (Su'en) beseeches his father, Enlil: "[W]hy have you turned away from Ur . . . ?" This contrasts with line 450, in which the son asks again but in which Enlil answers favorably. He blesses him and promises the city of Ur will be rebuilt splendidly (Michalowski).

For now, she maintains her silence. The section ends somewhat oddly with what seems to be an extension of the theme of YHWH's uniquely creative prowess vis-à-vis Babylon's gods: "It is I who created the smith . . . so it is I who create the instruments of havoc; no weapon formed against you shall succeed" (54:16–17). Talk of weapons of destruction and their creation is a rhetorically double-edged sword, so to speak. As well as offering comfort, it serves as a reminder of YHWH's admitted responsibility for Zion's destruction. He has shown himself as capable of wielding those swords against his own people as of withholding them. The very last verse of chapter 54, which is the last verse of the last section directed toward Zion, merges Zion and the "servants" of YHWH. Here she becomes "them," the masculine plural audience addressed throughout the chapters. Up to this point, the Servant and Zion have been kept quite distinct (while masculine singular and masculine plural addressees are occasionally combined as in chapter 43). It is as if her recalcitrance can be overcome by merging her with her more compliant sibling.

Second Isaiah has long been recognized as a response to the pained speech of Lamentations, as well as to many other texts. Its intertextual resonances extend broadly and deeply. That its poetic expression of hope is profoundly beautiful and moving is beyond question. The movement from the Prophets to Lamentations to Second Isaiah is psychologically adept as well. It charts common human experience from complacency to dis-ease to glimmers of hope. It is a psychologically astute and therapeutic movement except for the fact that at every step the dis-ease is meant to defend God by blaming humans. Even in the texts of hope, the primary goal remains the same. Brueggemann has noted a similar movement in the Psalter, resulting in an ultimately satisfying dialectic, even from the standpoint of the supplicant. In the conjunction of these texts, however, we do not see a return to complacency or equilibrium, not if our evaluation is interested in Zion's perspective.[13] More specifically, how does Second Isaiah rate qualitatively as a genuinely dialogic text, as a response to the protest tendered by Daughter Zion? God never really answers *the* question (though not explicitly Zion's question) of Lamentations: Why have you done this? In terms of divine self-expression, the Bible is always theodic. Its answer to this question is, inevitably (and this includes Second Isaiah's answer): "Hey, look at this other great thing I'm doing for you, or am about to do."

It is, in the end, an insufficient response to Lam 1–2 because it is ultimately a controlling discourse, not one that allows other voices any significant power or influence. Is YHWH in Second Isaiah contrite? Not exactly. Is his desire for reconciliation genuine? Perhaps. Does he have an agenda beyond the good of Daughter Zion? Most certainly. YHWH's discourse in Second Isaiah may be sympathetic, even kind at times, but it is not gen-

---

13. Even moving beyond Second Isaiah, in the postexilic texts, we do not see a return to "shalom." The Tanakh's movement, overall, tends toward discord.

uinely empathetic. Even his kindness is constrained by the demands of patriarchal hegemony—his love is boundless only within the given parameters of obedience and faithfulness. Integral to his promise is the insistence that from this point forward "all of your children will be disciples of YHWH" (54:13a). Insofar as they toe that line everyone will be happy (54:13b). As tender and lovely as is chapter 54's rhetoric, it is bent on figuring the divine/human relationship along the lines of a traditional colonial affiliation between patron and vassal, and privileging the male-divine relationship over the female-divine, the logocentric over the polyphonic.

> Second Isaiah does not maintain Lamentations' strong parallelism of function. This poet finally, like Jeremiah, calls the audience to identify with the male figure, not with Zion. The masculine plural audience is enmeshed with the servant, but separated from Zion rhetorically until the very last verse addressed to her, in which they seem to have become servants of YHWH *in* Zion (54:17). (Tull Willey 1995:202)

With the focus on masculine singular and masculine plural addressees, the rhetoric of Second Isaiah might be read as coaxing the people back to their abandoned and decimated "mother." She sits alone "back there" waiting for them. Of course some of the rhetoric is directed at her specifically, but much of it is about her children returning to her—a rather sly way of making the people feel emotionally caught up in contributing to her well-being.

Of course the males, while privileged over the females, are still subordinates in the prophet's theological configuration. Zion and her people will serve and obey; YHWH will love and protect. Other relational configurations are outside the discursive possibilities of the ideology of this text. It is no wonder that God's and Zion's voices cannot organically inhabit the same text. What the text reveals, counterintuitively for many of us, is that *God's love does have limits.* This may seem reasonable, especially in human terms—why should anyone love those who are not loyal to them? This is not a groundbreaking discovery, but it is instructive to delineate how the text actually lays this out, naturalizes it, and thereby hides it in plain view. This is not to let Zion off the hook. Answerability has been demanded of her for some worthy reasons. It is incumbent on her as a responsible and mature member of a relationship to attend to her shortcomings—such as her failure to do justice, especially for political expediency. But scholars have long been quick to side with God; Zion's responsibility for her downfall has been excessively championed. Insofar as we hearken to the demands for justice made of us, it is good practice, if nothing else, to tune our ears to a frequency that picks up the words of the marginalized. Zion's voice, as a female voice in a patriarchal text, as a lone voice that challenges the divine/prophetic discursive hegemony, is a good voice on which to practice. It teaches us to hear "outside the box." It can be scary because it puts love of justice above love of God, at least the god made in our (discursive) image. It is not a claim for "objective" reading, quite the opposite. It is an intentional reading that focuses on nondominant voices and ideologies. Nondominant does not mean "right" or "better"; it means lacking power and authority. My reading expressly chooses to try to redress the imbalances.

# 6

# Why Dialogic Reading Matters

*No place of grace for those who avoid the face; No time to rejoice for those who walk among noise and deny the voice.* (T. S. Eliot, "Ash Wednesday")

*For you, O Lord. With you. In you. Against you. Ani maamin, ani maamin. Hear us, O God, hear us.* (Elie Wiesel, *Ani Maamin*)

Bakhtin and Buber taught us to pay attention to the dialogism inherent in our sociocultural, including religious, discourses. For them, attending to the voices around us was an ethical and moral imperative. Voices intermingle in myriad discourses, including literature. Literature, however, as a mimetic discourse often reflects the monologic point of view of its creator, so it can be more or less dialogic according to Bakhtin's standards. (In my opinion it is impossible for any text to be wholly monologic, but literature is artistically richer when its voices are given freer rein.) Bakhtin did not recognize biblical discourse as particularly dialogic, but this is largely because, like so many others, he read it through the lens of the church's control of its interpretation. In other words, he understood it, for the most part, as the monologic "word of the father." But this says more about how biblical hermeneutics has been (and continues to be in many circles) exercised in a straitjacket. Political and ideological demands, in general, necessitate readings that uphold singular theological beliefs. However, as many are beginning to recognize, the Bible is rich with voices—independent, contrary, "free" voices. The vast diversity of biblical voices ensures that they find resonance in the lives of real persons. When we consider it our moral duty to give full recognition to all voices in the text (even those that morally repel us, and that we might finally part company with), we are practicing a dialogic ethic that one can hope has real-life consequences.

As is well known by now, reading is an ethical activity—textual rhetoric forces us to make choices, choices that reflect who we are and what we value. What does it say about what we value when we read Lam 1–2 and yet side with the prophets against Daughter Zion? It is an interesting question, and one, I would bet, that rarely gets asked. Of course, we need to ask ourselves the same question if we side indiscriminately against the divine voice. When we find the answer, we can decide honestly if the answer reflects the kind of person we want to be.

Naturally enough given his literary bent, Bakhtin focused on how form/genre reflects dialogic realities. We manage raw data through formal categories, which are not merely abstract formalities but live (and die) in flesh-and-blood contexts. They evolve according to the needs of their consumers. Genres are rarely pure or monological but are sometimes more explicitly or dramatically forced to incorporate diverse voices—during times of trauma or social upheaval, for example. At these times, new possibilities for understanding the world break into view. In Lamentations, the combination of lament, dirge, and city lament creates a new type of lament that proffers a theological point of view that is fundamentally at odds (although not necessarily different in particulars) with typical laments, and diametrically opposed to the ideology of the prophetic use of the marriage metaphor. From this combination emerges a raw, experiential discourse that makes ethical demands upon us, beginning with the demand simply to listen and hear. If we listen, what we hear is anger, betrayal, and suffering beyond comprehension or value. After listening, the next step is to decide upon a response. With whom do we place our allegiance? With the victim? With the powers that be? With both in varying degrees? With neither? Surely different contexts will demand different answers. Making that call is simply part of the ethical maturity that life demands of us. Our choice will consequently dictate where our feet take us and what our hands do when we get there.

In chapter 3, I offered an example of how taking note of generic inflections reveals theological tracings that often remain implicit otherwise. Whereas in the prophetic texts, the divine voice dominates every other voice in its purview, in Lam 1–2, Daughter Zion's point of view is dominant largely because the DV—formally a divine rhetoric—sides with her (especially in Lam 2). But her discourse is scattered with references to the prophetic ideology that blames her for her situation. She does not exactly deny the divine point of view but accentuates her suffering over her culpability. Generically, the divine voice and the supplicant's voice are more comfortably integrated in the lament psalms. But one result of the rupture of 587 B.C.E. was to split these voices—prophets versus Daughter Zion—into warring parties that for the time being anyway cannot be integrated without threatening the integrity of both. While in most lament psalms some blame could be heaped upon YHWH without dismantling belief in his ultimate justice, in the prophetic use of the marriage metaphor YHWH's justice is guarded at all costs. In Lam 1–2 the people cannot accept the consequences of acquiescing to belief in God's justice without undermining their own integrity. In the case of Lam 1–2, the apparent dominance of Daughter Zion's voice seems to serve a crucial ethical purpose—to offer a counterstory and bolster a voice that is in danger of falling into the abyss, a voice that has been brutalized first by prophetic pronouncements and delivered a final blow by God's hand. In other words, a relative monologism in this case provides a necessary corrective to the crushing monologism of prophetic discourse. Of course, reading the Bible dialogically means juxtaposing the two books and taking account of both voices. The Bible courageously offers both voices to us, so we should not be shy about jumping into the fray with them, with the goal of ultimately inviting more voices to our own tables.

The purpose of reading dialogically is to attune ourselves to the multiplicity of voices that surround us at every moment and to recognize that just as the Bible honors (although individual voices within it may not!) "counter" voices, so should we. The voice of Daughter Zion not only attacks God, but in doing so challenges divine authority, in general, and the theological status quo of her world. Further, while Daughter Zion's rhetoric may pose a challenge to her own world, it likely poses an even greater challenge to our status quo than the world in which she lived. Canonical diversity attests to a willingness on the part of the ancients to rock the boat. Countervoices have a greater prominence in biblical texts than we (especially Christians) have generally recognized. It has taken over a century of critical biblical scholarship to begin to hear Daughter Zion's words on their own terms, but that does not mean she has not been speaking. For those who take the issue of biblical authority (however defined) seriously, it seems an ethical imperative that a voice deemed worthy of canonization not be de facto excluded. After all, to pay attention is the only thing Daughter Zion asks and the least we can do.

But how does God do on this score? Does he "pay attention"? In Second Isaiah, God acknowledges the voice of Daughter Zion and, at least tacitly, the fact that he has gravely wounded her. While we might find God's response to be lacking under the circumstances, we can take heart from the fact that Second Isaiah's discourse attests to an understanding of the importance of dialogue and reciprocity. Still, it seems, in the end, that God's attempts at reconciliation fall short—Daughter Zion does not respond to God's overtures, while the "Servant" does. A dialogic ethic necessitates honoring both responses, which have their own internal logic and integrity. Second Isaiah is to be commended for including more voices than its prophetic predecessors, but, in the end, I read God's response as a failure for Daughter Zion, at least. The sad truth is that sometimes we are damaged beyond healing—at least if by "healing" we mean a return to the status quo. We may find a way to go on, but we may never be reconciled to what happened to us, or to the party who inflicted suffering on us. I can imagine that as the *golah* community listened to Second Isaiah's attempt at conveying a message of comfort, some felt healing creep back into their bones (à la Ezekiel's "dry bones"), but there were surely those damaged beyond reconciliation (or resurrection).

Similarly, as E. Berkovits notes in his post-Holocaust theology, some survivors of the Shoah irrevocably lost their faith to the crematoria of Auschwitz. He enjoins us to honor the "holy disbelief" of those whose faith went up in smoke as a mysterious act of faith in its own right. In a post-Holocaust (and post-9/11) world we may feel abandoned by God, but the Bible continues to be a powerful testimony to the human will to survive and make meaning out of the raw material of existence. Every voice in the book has a role to play in that task. Dialogue does not mean everything is "fixed," but dialogue is our best hope. Daughter Zion in these texts is not healed, but the dialogue continues through interpretation, as we struggle to find better responses to her suffering. Many readers of the Bible will find their truth in Daughter Zion's words at some point in their lives. As a community of readers we have to support that possibility by first hearing Zion, and then hearing those readers.

How might God have been a more responsible listener? To start, rather than continue to sidestep issues of divine culpability, he might have explicitly admitted that he failed in his duty as a husband. The rabbis seemed to understand the need for a divine declaration of guilt. In the twenty-fourth *petihta* of *Lamentations Rabbah*, the rabbis merge the voice of God and voice of Daughter Zion as God weeps and laments the pain of the loss of his own children: "O children of mine, where are you? O priests of mine, where are you? O you who love me, where are you? What shall I do for you? I warned you, but you did not repent."[1] While still reliant on a retributive theology, this heartfelt rendering shows God's empathy with Daughter Zion, and it suggests an implicit acknowledgment that he has allowed his anger too free a rein. A divine empathetic response is missing in Lamentations and cannot even be said to exist in Second Isaiah, for that matter. Still, in this midrashic interpolation God does not exactly admit to fault—ultimate blame remains with the people for not listening. What God is unwilling or unable to do in the midrashic imagination, the rabbis still manage to express through the use of the patriarchs and Rachel who indict God before a tribunal and win their case. According to the rabbis, we are in good company when we take God to task for his lapses in judgment. The rabbis commission Abraham to bring a case against God, whereby Abraham refutes and shames all the witnesses God calls against Israel—specifically Torah itself, as well as each letter of the alphabet—into silence. God's accusations against the people are not convincing to Abraham as he laments the suffering his people have endured. When Jacob takes the stand, he acknowledges the diffi-

---

1. I appreciate Tod Linafelt's (*Surviving Lamentations*) insightful exposition of this *petihta*, which led me to give it a closer look.

culties inherent in child-rearing, but for him that does not excuse God's abandonment of his children. Even God's own angels are convinced enough to accuse God of breaking the covenant. What all these chastising voices raised against God seem to be eliciting is divine acknowledgment of fault—repentance, even.

The notion of divine repentance is, to some, unthinkable by definition. Ultimate power eschews repentance, and most of us do not like to entertain the idea that our ostensibly wise leaders are fallible. However, without the possibility of repentance, dialogue is crippled from the start. This entrenched dynamic is part and parcel of the normative hermeneutic model, but one that has outlived its usefulness and must be resisted. The rabbis make a good start when they paint the patriarchs as demonstrating a better sense of loyalty than God himself. This bold observation actually points up one of the reasons that a reading that takes into account diverse voices is so essential. Taking into full account Daughter Zion's story means admitting that sometimes humans demonstrate more moral integrity than God. As illustration, the rabbis in *Petihta* 24 have Moses go to Babylon to liberate the exiles because God will not. God does not send Moses on this second exodus—Moses takes it upon himself.

The potentially provocative image of the patriarchs taking over God's responsibilities represents a powerful rhetorico-theological strategy that emphasizes human responsibility—when God does not seem to be exercising justice, it does not mean that we shouldn't. In fact, unequivocally expressing faith in the biblical God as a moral exemplar can have profoundly negative implications.

> Because biblical texts are powerful artistic works and honored as sacred texts in communities of faith, they have great potential to sanction violence and abuse and, at the least, leave unchallenged the violence and abuse among us. In the United States these texts are especially dangerous because this culture is saturated in violence. (O'Connor 2000:117)

An example of the ways the Bible can sanction violence that is particularly apt considering our focus on the marriage metaphor can be found in the advice priests, pastors, and even friends sometimes give to women suffering from spousal abuse. Carole Bohn offers compelling evidence of the severity of this problem.

> [I]t is quite common for women who seek counsel from ministers to receive some variation on advice reflecting the minister's belief in a theology of ownership, advice such as
>
> —Marriage is sacred and you must do whatever you can to hold it together.
> —Your husband is the head of your household; do what he tells you and he won't need to resort to violence.
> —You must have done something to provoke him; go home and mend your ways so he will not need to behave in this manner. (106–7)

This is the kind of situation we risk when we uncritically accept God's narrative of the events recounted in many prophetic texts. "If God can be 'cruel to be kind' then this could be taken as justification for similar behaviour in the human sphere" (Guest: 431). Brueggemann concurs, emphasizing that "pastoral work must be enormously attentive to power relations and the ways in which hegemony is imposed and what it costs to break out of that hegemony" (2001:25). Fretheim provides, in my opinion, an example of dangerous naïveté in this regard. He employs the marriage metaphor to remind us of the relational concern and foundation of God's judging activities: "When thinking of God as judge, remember that the judge behind the bench is the spouse of the accused in the dock" (160). For Fretheim, this conjures a positive image—the god who judges is ostensibly the loving spouse. Apparently, this should reassure us. Rather, isn't this image exactly the problem? Could such an image ever be a trope for a healthy relationship? It does not seem too radical to observe that husbands should not be their wives' judges, they should be their partners! Our need to insist upon God's goodness to the exclusion of any negative traits is entirely understandable—it is as if our very lives depend upon it. But might not our lives equally depend upon reading this influential text more honestly and critically? Isn't O'Connor's frank though difficult reading of God's brutality more conducive to honesty in our ethical dealings with one another? "The mere accumulation of violent deeds here and elsewhere implies that, if this is punishment, it exceeds all bounds, all proportionality to the sin. The God who should protect and cherish her has battered and harmed her in every way short of killing her" (2002: 111). Alas, this is the more likely outcome when the husband plays the judge. What we need more of, in Christian theology at least, is what W. Farley calls "tragic vision." This vision provides an important corrective to Christianity's comic theological trajectory that insists that at the beginning of most suffering is sin, and at the end of all suffering is God's redemptive activity. Some suffering, what Farley calls "radical suffering," is both guiltless and simply too great to be justified by Christianity's expiatory and eschatological understanding of history.

O'Connor's theological reading of Lamentations confronts squarely the abuses with which God has afflicted Daughter Zion, but in the end she, like many, is uncomfortable with an abusive-god theology such as that proposed by David Blumenthal for the following reason.

> If God abuses and cruelly and violently controls us, then it is surely fine for humans to be abusive and violently controlling as well. The ways we imagine God encourage, support, and affirm our own behavior. An abusing God leaves abuse and violence unchallenged in families, churches, and nations. If God is abusive, then God is unjust and immoral. If God is abusive, victims of abuse are without refuge, tyrants and bullies cannot be restrained, and love can never be trusted. (110)

I agree wholeheartedly with the first half of her statement. We must beware of a God who abuses because such an image has the potential to sanction oppressive human structures. But the fact is that God in the Bible *sometimes* (and this is a qualifier Blumenthal stresses) abuses. The issue is not to find some way around that fact, but what we do with it. We must bring voices forward to challenge God's abusing voice. We must not accept his hegemony as narrated uncritically. *The dialogic structure of the canon gives us sanction for resisting seemingly irresistible power in our own contexts.* Which brings me to the latter half of O'Connor's statement—even though (not "if") God is sometimes abusive, it does not follow that victims are without refuge and bullies go unrestrained. As Abraham and Moses illustrate in the imagination of the rabbis, it is *our* responsibility to protect victims of abuse. Tragic suffering does not require atonement, it requires defiance—in the form of human compassion (Farley: 29). As W. Brueggemann notes, if we ignore or explain away the difficult issues raised by biblical countervoices then we will not have the will to pose the hard questions of justice, those which faith demands we pose, even before the throne of God himself (1986:64).

It is beyond question for many biblical theologians that human sin sanctions divine wrath (although many today will treat the notion of divine wrath figuratively). To start posing the "hard questions" we should define what we mean by sin before deciding that committing it deserves God's wrath and our righteous anger. For the prophets (not to mention the Deuteronomist), sin seems to boil down to disloyalty or disobedience toward God. This understanding of the nature of sin first and foremost valorizes exclusive loyalty as the supreme virtue: "You shall have no gods before me" is the basis for the covenant established between YHWH and the people. I wonder, though, for all its hype, if loyalty in the sense of exclusivity is a trait we want to continue to valorize? R. Schwartz has called attention to the danger of the Bible's emphasis on exclusivity in the construction of identity. When we make hard-and-fast choices, we are by necessity setting ourselves against (one) an other. Is it really so important that the people make a choice between YHWH and the "Queen of Heaven"? Typically, we accept uncritically that something tremendous is at stake in this choice. Today, we might hear our rabbis, ministers, and priests speak of "idols" metaphorically as standing for everything detrimental to the "good life," but that is surely not how the ancient worshipers experienced their cultic practices, and we probably need to let our prejudices go if all they do is lead us to inflexibility (and ultimately violence) in our dealings with one another. Now more than ever, we are learning what is at stake in this regard.

Currently, human beings are caught in a religious conflict of global proportions that attests to the possible injurious effects of such rigidity. On every side there are powerful people that think they own the exclusive license to play God and punish the "evildoers." This dynamic is at work on the more personal level as well. Gerald West, working out of his South African context, notes the damage done to those suffering from HIV/AIDS by a theological system that unequivocally upholds a belief in God's goodness and views human suffering as a mark of divine justice. Instead, West has implemented Bible study for AIDS sufferers that uses lamentation (Job mostly) as a way of providing a voice for these mostly intensely pious people whose situations are only exacerbated by traditional theodic understandings of God's providence.[2] The success he reports about this experiment confirms Brueggemann's now well-known appeal that Christians take better advantage of the psychological and spiritual benefits that can accrue from the expression of "angry" theological speech in certain circumstances (1986). Furthermore, the theological notion of forced obedience through a system of reward and punishment leaves little room for the human responsibility and initiative necessary to protect the God-abandoned (Plaskow: 131).

Finally, If I am reading the god in these particular texts correctly, why continue to turn to this book for moral sustenance? This brings us back to some of the points I made in the introductory chapter. The Bible continues to be revered by countless people and communities—I happen to think for good reason, but admittedly not the reason many think. The Bible's authority for me rests in its ability to mirror the diversity and complexity of human existence. It brings together in one book voices with, at the most extreme, diametrically opposed worldviews. And the books it contains do not come with headers cautioning that this particular voice should be censored, and that voice embraced. And rather than expunge, whitewash, or ignore the "dangerous" books as some are wont to do (not least some feminist critics), I agree with O'Connor wholeheartedly when she says:

> To excise the difficult texts erases possibilities of the texts to mirror present horrors, saves us from having to grapple with our own abuse and violence, and erases the cultural realities out of which the Bible emerged. (O'Connor 2003:118)

Rather, let us embrace and resist, rejoice and weep with, and, mostly, listen respectfully to what these voices have to say for themselves.

---

2. Presentation at the Society of Biblical Literature Annual Meeting, 2006.

# Works Cited

Abma, Richtse. 1999. *Bonds of Love: Methodic Studies of Prophetic Texts with Marriage Imagery. Isaiah 50:1–3 and 54:1–10, Hosea 1–3, Jeremiah 2–3.* Studia Semantica Neerlandica. Assan, Netherlands: Van Gorcum.

Austin, John Langshaw. 1962. *How to Do Things with Words.* Cambridge: Harvard University Press.

Bakhtin, Mikhail M. 1981. *The Dialogic Imagination.* University of Texas Press Slavic Series 1. Austin: University of Texas Press.

———. 1984. *Problems of Dostoevsky's Poetics.* Edited and translated by Caryl Emerson. Minneapolis: University of Minnesota Press.

———. 1986. *Speech Genres and Other Late Essays.* Edited by Michael Holquist and Caryl Emerson. Translated by Vern G. McGee. Austin: University of Texas Press.

———. 1990. *Art and Answerability: Early Philosophical Essays by M. M. Bakhtin.* Edited by Mikhail Bakhtin, Michael Holquist, and Vadim Liapunov. Translated by Kenneth Brostrom. Austin: University of Texas Press.

Bal, Mieke. 1987. *Lethal Love: Feminist Literary Readings of Biblical Love Stories.* Bloomington: Indiana University Press.

Bauer, Angela M. 1999. *Gender in the Book of Jeremiah: A Feminist-Literacy Reading.* New York: Peter Lang.

Baumann, Gerlinde. 2003. *Love and Violence: Marriage as Metaphor for the Relationship between YHWH and Israel in the Prophetic Books.* Translated by Linda Maloney. Collegeville, MN: Liturgical Press.

Benveniste, Emile. 1971. *Problems in General Linguistics.* Miami: University of Miami Press.

Berkovits, Eliezer. 1973. *Faith after the Holocaust.* New York: Ktav.

Berlin, Adele. 2002. *Lamentations.* Old Testament Library. Louisville: Westminster John Knox Press.

Berquist, Jon. 1996. Postcolonialism and Imperial Motives for Canonization. *Semeia* 75:15–35.

Biddle, Mark E. 1996. Lady Zion's Alter Egos: Isaiah 47.1–15 and 57.6–13 as Structural Counterparts. Pages 124–39 in *New Visions of Isaiah.* Edited by Marvin A. Sweeney and Roy F. Melugin. Journal for the Study of the Old Testament: Supplement Series 214. Sheffield: Sheffield Academic Press.

Bloch, Maurice. 1974. Symbols, Song, Dance, and Features of Articulation. *Archives europeenes de sociologie* 15:55–81.

Bloom, Harold. 1973. *The Anxiety of Influence: A Theory of Poetry.* New York: Oxford University Press.

Blount, Brian K., Walter Brueggemann, and William C. Placher. 2002. *Struggling with Scripture*. Louisville: Westminster John Knox Press.

Blumenthal, David. 1993. *Facing the Abusing God*. Louisville: Westminster John Knox Press.

Bohn, Carole R. 1989. Dominion to Rule: The Roots and Consequences of a Theology of Ownership. Pages 105–16 in *Christianity, Patriarchy, and Abuse: A Feminine Critique*. Edited by Joanne Carlson Brown and Carole R. Bohn. Cleveland: Pilgrim Press.

Brenner, Athalya. 1994. On Prophetic Propaganda and the Politics of "Love." Pages 87–107 in *Reflections on Theology and Gender*. Edited by Athalya Brenner and Fokkelien van Dijk-Hemmes. Kampen, Netherlands: Kok Pharos.

Brown, Sally A., and Patrick D. Miller. 2005. *Lament: Reclaiming Practices in Pulpit, Pew, and Public Square*. Louisville: Westminster John Knox Press.

Brueggemann, Walter. 1986. The Costly Loss of Lament. *Journal for the Study of the Old Testament* 36:57–71.

———. 1997. *Theology of the Old Testament: Testimony, Dispute, Advocacy*. Minneapolis: Fortress Press.

———. 2000. Biblical Theology Appropriately Postmodern. Pages 97–108 in *Jews, Christians, and the Theology of the Hebrew Scriptures*. Edited by Alice O. Bellis and Joel S. Kaminsky. Society of Biblical Literature Symposium Series 8. Atlanta: Society of Biblical Literature.

———. 2001. Voice as Counter to Violence. *Calvin Theological Journal* 36:22–33.

Buber, Martin. 1958. *I and Thou*. Translated by Ronald Gregor Smith. New York: Scribner's Sons.

———. 1960. *Prophetic Faith*. Translated by C. Witten-Davies. New York: Harper and Row.

———. 1964. *Werke II*. Vol. 2: *Schriften zur Bibel*. Heidelberg: Lambert Schneider.

———. 1965. The Word That Is Spoken. Pages xx–xxx in *The Knowledge of Man*. Edited by Maurice Friedman. Translated by Maurice Friedman and Ronald Gregor Smith. New York: Harper and Row.

———. 1967. *Kingship of God*. Translated by R. Scheimann. New York: Harper and Row.

Bulhan, Hussein Abdilahi. 1985. *Frantz Fanon and the Psychology of Oppression*. New York: Plenum Press.

Buss, Martin J. 1999. *Form Criticism in Its Context*. Journal for the Study of the Old Testament: Supplement Series 274. Sheffield: Sheffield Academic Press.

Claassens, Juliana. 2003. Biblical Theology as Dialogue: Continuing the Conversation on Mikhail Bakhtin and the Biblical Theology. *Journal of Biblical Literature* 122:127–44.

Coleridge, Mark. 2003. Life in the Crypt or Why Bother with Biblical Studies? In *Biblical Studies Alternatively: An Introductory Reader*. Upper Saddle River, NJ: Prentice Hall.

Cosgrove, Charles. 2004. Toward a Postmodern Hermeneutica Sacra: Guiding Considerations in Choosing between Competing Plausible Interprestations of Scripture. Pages 39–61 in *The Meanings We Choose: Hermeneutical Ethics, Indeterminacy, and the Conflict of Interpretations*. Edited by Charles Cosgrove. London: T&T Clark.

Darr, Kathryn Pfisterer. 1992. Ezekiel's Justifications of God: Teaching Troubling Texts. *Journal for the Study of the Old Testament* 55:97–117.

Davidson, R. 1985. *Jeremiah II with Lamentations*. Edinburgh: St. Andrew's Press.

Day, Peggy. 2000. The Bitch Had It Coming to Her: Rhetoric and Interpretation in Ezekiel 16. *Biblical Interpretation* 8:231–54.

De Moor, Johannes C. 2003. Theodicy in the Texts of Ugarit. Pages 108–50 in *Theodicity in the World of the Bible*. Edited by Johannes C. de Moor and Antti Laato. Leiden: Brill.

Diamond, A. R. Pete, and K. M. O'Connor. 1996. Unfaithful Passions: Coding Women Coding Men in Jeremiah 2–3 (4:2). *Biblical Interpretation* 4:288–310.

Diaz-Diocaretz, Myriam. 1989. Bakhtin, Discourse, and Feminist Theory. *Critical Studies* 1:121–39.

Dobbs-Allsopp, F. W. 1993. *Weep O Daughter Zion: A Study of the City-Lament Genre in the Hebrew Bible*. Biblica et Orientalia 44. Rome: Editrice Pontifico Istituto Biblico.

———. 2002. *Lamentations*. Louisville: Westminster John Knox Press.

Dobbs-Allsopp, F. W., and Tod Linafelt. 2001. The Rape of Zion in Thr 1, 10. *Zeitschrift für die alttestamentliche Wissenschaft* 113:77–81.

Domeris, William R. 1999. When Metaphor Becomes Myth: A Socio-linguistic Reading of Jeremiah. Pages 244–62 in *Troubling Jeremiah*. Edited by A. R. Pete Diamond, Louis Stulman, and Kathleen O'Connor. Journal for the Study of the Old Testament: Supplement Series 260. Sheffield: Sheffield Academic Press.

Dube, Musa W. 2002. Postcoloniality, Feminist Spaces, and Religion. Pages 100–120 in *Postcolonialism, Feminism, and Religious Discourse*. Edited by Laura E. Donaldson and Kwok Pui-Lan. New York: Routledge.

Edelstein, Marilyn. 1992. Metaphor, Meta-Narrative, and Mater-Narrative in Kristeva's "Stabat Mater." Pages 27–52 in *Body/Text in Julia Kristeva: Religion, Women, and Psychoanalysis*. Edited by David Crownfield. Albany: SUNY Press.

Emerson, Caryl, and Gary S. Morson. 1990. *Mikhail Bakhtin: Creation of a Prosaics*. Stanford, CA: Stanford University Press.

Exum, J. Cheryl. 1996. *Plotted, Shot, and Painted: Cultural Representations of Biblical Women*. Gender, Culture, Theory 3. Sheffield: Sheffield Academic Press.

Farley, Wendy. 1990. *Tragic Vision and Divine Compassion*. Louisville: Westminster John Knox Press.

Fishelov, David. 1993. *Metaphors of Genre: The Role of Analogies in Genre Theory*. University Park: Pennsylvania State University Press.

Fowler, Alastair. 1982. *Kinds of Literature: An Introduction to the Theory of Genres and Modes*. Cambridge: Harvard University Press.

Fretheim, Terence E. 2005. *God and World in the Old Testament: A Relational Theology*. Nashville: Abingdon Press.

Galambush, Julie. 1992. *Jerusalem in the Book of Ezekiel: The City as Yahweh's Wife*. SBLDS 130. Atlanta: Scholars Press.

Gandhi, Leela. 1998. *Postcolonial Theory*. New York: Columbia University Press.

Gerstenberger, Erhard. 1998. *Psalms*. Forms of the Old Testament Literature 14. Grand Rapids: Eerdmans.

Gottwald, Norman. 1992. Social Class and Ideology in Isaiah 40–55: An Eagletonian Reading. *Semeia* 59:43–57.

Graetz, Naomi. 1999. Jerusalem the Widow. *Shofar* 17:16–24.

Green, Barbara. 2000. *Mikhail Bakhtin and Biblical Scholarship: An Introduction*. Semeia Studies 38. Atlanta: Society of Biblical Literature.

———. 2003. *King Saul's Asking*. Collegeville, MN: Liturgical Press.

———. 2005. *Jonah's Journey*. Collegeville, MN: Liturgical Press.

Griffiths, Gareth. 1994. The Myth of Authenticity: Representation, Discourse, and Social Practice. Pages 70–85 in *De-Scribing Empire: Post-colonialism and Textuality*. Edited by Alan Lawson and Chris Tiffin. New York: Routledge.

Guest, Deryn. 1999. Hiding behind the Naked Woman in Lamentations. *Biblical Interpretation* 7, no. 4: 413–48.

Hajdukowski-Ahmed. 1990. Bakhtin and Feminism: Two Solitudes. *Critical Studies* 2:153–63.

Harrison, R. K. 1973. *Jeremiah and Lamentations: An Introduction and Commentary*. London: Tyndale Press.

Heim, Knut. 1999. The Personification of Jerusalem and the Drama of Her Bereavement in Lamentations. Pages 129–69 in *Zion, City of Our God*. Edited by Richard Hess and Gordon Wenham. Grand Rapids: Eerdmans.

Hillers, Delbert R. 1972. *Lamentations: Introduction, Translation, and Notes*. Anchor Bible. Garden City, NY: Doubleday.

Holquist, Michael. 1999. Introduction. Pages ix–xlix in *Art and Answerability: Early Philosophical Essays*. Edited by Michael Holquist and Vadim Liapunov. Austin: University of Texas Press.

Irigaray, Luce. 1993. Divine Women. Pages 57–72 in *Sexes and Genealogies*. Translated by Gillian C. Gill. New York: Columbia University Press.

Jenny, Laurent. 1982. The Strategy of Form. Pages 34–63 in *French Literary Theory Today: A Reader*. Edited by Tzvetan Todorov. Cambridge: Cambridge University Press.

Johnson, Mark, and George Lakoff. 1981. Conceptual Metaphor in Everyday Language. Pages 286–329 in *Philosophical Perspectives on Metaphor*. Edited by Mark Johnson. Minneapolis: University of Minneapolis Press.

———. 2003. *Metaphors We Live By*. Chicago: University of Chicago Press.

Jones, Serene. 1993. This God Which Is Not One: Irigaray and Barth on the Divine. Pages 109–41 in *Transfigurations: Theology and the French Feminists*. Edited by C. W. Maggie Kim et al. Minneapolis: Fortress Press.

Kaiser, Barbara Bakke. 1987. Poet as "Female Impersonator": The Image of Daughter Zion as Speaker in Biblical Poems of Suffering. *The Journal of Religion* (April): 164–82.

Kanneh, Kadiatu. 1995. Feminism and the Colonial Body. Pages 346–48 in *The Post-colonial Studies Reader*. Edited by Bill Ashcroft, Gareth Griffiths, and Helen Tiffin. New York: Routledge.

Keefe, Alice. 2001. *Woman's Body and the Social Body in Hosea*. Gender, Culture, Theory 10. London: Sheffield Academic Press.

Kepnes, Steven. 1992. *The Text as Thou: Martin Buber's Dialogical Hermeneutics and Narrative Theology*. Indianapolis: Indiana University Press.

Knight, Henry F. 2000. *Confessing Christ in a Post-Holocaust World: A Midrashic Experiment*. Westport, CT: Greenwood Press.

Kristeva, Julia. 1980. Word, Dialogue, and the Novel. Pages 64–91 in *Desire in Language: A Semitic Approach to Literature and Art*. New York: Columbia University Press.

Kwok Pui-Lan. 2005. *Postcolonial Imagination and Feminist Theology*. Louisville: Westminster John Knox Press.

Labahn, Antje. 2003. Metaphor and Intertextuality: "Daughter of Zion" as a Test Case. *Scandinavian Journal of the Old Testament* 17:49–67.

Lakoff, Robin. 2004. *Language and Woman's Place: Text and Commentaries*. Edited by Mary Bucholtz. 2nd ed. New York: Oxford University Press.

Lanahan, William. 1974. The Speaking Voice in the Book of Lamentations. *Journal of Biblical Literature* 93:41–49.

Landy, Francis. 1995. In the Wilderness of Speech: Problems of Metaphor in Hosea. *Biblical Interpretation* 3:35–59.

Laytner, Anson. 1998. *Arguing with God: A Jewish Tradition*. Lanham, MD: Jason Aronson.

Leclerc, Annie. 1992. Woman's Word. Pages 362–65 in *Feminist Philosophies: Problems, Theories, and Applications*. Edited by Janet A. Kournay, James P. Sterba, and Rosemarie Tong. Englewood Cliffs, NJ: Prentice Hall.

Lee, Nancy C. 1999. Exposing a Buried Subtext in Jeremiah and Lamentations: Going after Baal and Abel. Pages 87–122 in *Troubling Jeremiah*. Edited by A. R. Diamond, Louis Stulman, and Kathleen O'Connor. Journal for the Study of the Old Testament: Supplement Series 260. Sheffield: Sheffield Academic Press.

———. 2002. *The Singers of Lamentations: Cities under Siege, from Ur to Jerusalem to Sarajevo*. Biblical Interpretation Series 60. Leiden: Brill.

Lorde, Audre. 2003. The Master's Tools Will Never Dismantle the Master's House. Pages 25–28 in *Feminist Postcolonial Theory: A Reader*. Edited by Reina Lewis and Sara Mills. New York: Taylor and Francis.

MacIntyre, Alasdair C. 1984. *After Virtue: A Study in Moral Theory*. Notre Dame, IN: Notre Dame Press.

Maier, Christl. 1998. Die Klage der Tochter Zion. *Berliner Theologische Zeitschrift* 15:176–89.

Mandolfo, Carleen. 2002. *God in the Dock: Dialogic Tension in the Psalms of Lament*. Sheffield: Sheffield Academic Press.

Michalowski, Piotr. 1989. *The Lamentations Over the Destruction of Sumer and Ur*. Winona Lake, IN: Eisenbrauns.

Nelson, Hilde L. 2001. *Damaged Identities, Narrative Repair*. Ithaca, NY: Cornell University Press.

Newsom, Carol A. 1997. Women and the Discourse of Patriarchal Wisdom. Pages 116–31 in *Reading Bibles, Writing Bodies: Identity and the Book*. Edited by Timothy K. Beal and David M. Gunn. London: Routledge.

———. 2003. *The Book of Job: A Contest of Moral Imaginations*. New York: Oxford University Press.

O'Connor, Kathleen M. 1999a. Speak Tenderly to Jerusalem: Second Isaiah's Reception and Use of Daughter Zion. *The Princeton Seminary Bulletin* 20:281–94.

———. 1999b. The Tears of God and Divine Character. Pages 387–401 in *Troubling Jeremiah*. Edited by A. R. Diamond, Louis Stulman, and Kathleen O'Connor. Journal for the Study of the Old Testament: Supplement Series 260. Sheffield: Sheffield Academic Press.

———. 2001. Jeremiah. In *The New Interpreter's Study Bible: Isaiah–Ezekiel*. Vol. 6. Edited by David L. Peterson, Christopher R. Seitz, and Gene M. Tucker. Nashville: Abingdon Press.

———. 2002. *Lamentations and the Tears of the World*. Maryknoll, NY: Orbis.

Pardes, Ilana. 1992. *Countertraditions in the Bible: A Feminist Approach*. Boston: Harvard University Press.

Patrick, Dale. 1999. *The Rhetoric of Revelation in the Hebrew Bible*. Minneapolis: Fortress Press.

Pham, Xuan Huong Thi. 1999. *Mourning in the Ancient Near East and the Hebrew Bible*. Journal for the Study of the Old Testament: Supplement Series 302. Sheffield: Sheffield Academic Press.

Phoca, Sophia, and Rebecca Wright. 1999. *Introducing Postfeminism*. London: Icon Books.

Plaskow, Judith. 1991. *Standing Again at Sinai: Judaism from a Feminist Perspective*. New York: HarperCollins.

Rich, Adrienne. 2003. Notes towards a Politics of Location. Pages 29–42 in *Feminist Postcolonial Theory: A Reader*. Edited by Reina Lewis and Sara Mills. New York: Taylor and Francis.

Ricoeur, Paul. 1980. Toward a Hermeneutic of the Idea of Revelation. Pages 73–118 in *Essays on Biblical Interpretation*. Edited by L. S. Mudge. Philadelphia: Fortress Press.

———. 1998. Metaphor and the Central Problem of Hermeneutics. Pages 194–202 in *Continental Philosophy: An Anthology*. Edited by W. McNeill and K. Feldman. Malden, MA: Blackwell.

Sartre, Jean-Paul. 1969. *Being and Nothingness*. London: Taylor and Francis.

Sawyer, John F. A. 1989. Daughter Zion and Servant of the Lord in Isaiah: A Comparison. *Journal for the Study of the Old Testament* 44:89–107.

Schüssler Fiorenza, Elisabeth. 1999. *Rhetoric and Ethic: The Politics of Biblical Studies*. Minneapolis: Fortress Press.

Schwartz, Regina M. 1997. *The Curse of Cain: The Violent Legacy of Monotheism*. Chicago: University of Chicago Press.

Scott, James. 1990. *Domination and the Arts of Resistance: Hidden Transcripts*. New Haven: Yale University Press.

Seow, Choon-Leong. 1985. A Textual Note on Lamentations 1:20. *CBQ* 47:416–19.

Sheffield, Carole. 1992. Sexual Terrorism. Pages 60–72 in *Feminist Philosophies: Problems, Theories, and Applications*. Edited by Janet A. Kournay, James P. Sterba, and Rosemarie Tong. Englewood Cliffs, NJ: Prentice Hall.

Sherwood, Yvonne. 1996. *Prostitute and the Prophet: Hosea's Marriage in Literary-Theoretical Perspective*. Sheffield: Sheffield Academic Press.

———. 2004. Jacques Derrida and Biblical Studies. *SBL Forum* 2 (November).

Shields, Mary E. 1995. Circumcision of the Prostitute: Gender, Sexuality, and the Call to Repentance in Jeremiah 3:1–4:4. *Biblical Interpretation* 3:61–74.

———. 1998. Multiple Exposures: Body Rhetoric and Gender Characterization in Ezekiel 16. *Journal of Feminist Studies in Religion* 14:5–18.

Siegelman, Ellen Y. 1990. *Metaphor and Meaning in Psychotherapy*. New York: Guilford Press.

Smith-Christopher, Daniel. 2002. *A Biblical Theology of Exile*. Minneapolis: Fortress Press.

Sommer, Benjamin D. 1998. *A Prophet Reads Scripture: Allusion in Isaiah 40–66*. Stanford, CA: Stanford University Press.

Spivak, Gayatri Chakravorty. 1983. Displacement and the Discourse of Women. Pages 169–95 in *Displacement: Derrida and After*. Edited by M. Krupnick. Bloomington, IN: Indiana University Press.

Tull, Patricia K. 2003. Rhetorical Criticism and Beyond in Second Isaiah. Pages 326–34 in *The Changing Face of Form Criticism for the Twenty-First Century*. Edited by Ehud Ben Zvi and Martin Sweeney. Grand Rapids: Eerdmans.

Tull Willey, Patricia K. 1995. The Servant of YHWH and Daughter Zion: Alternating

Visions of YHWH's Community. Pages 267–303 in *Society of Biblical Literature Seminar Papers*. Society of Biblical Literature Seminary Papers. Atlanta: Scholars Press.

———. 1997. *Remember the Former Things: The Recollection of Previous Texts in Second Isaiah*. SBLDS 161. Atlanta: Scholars Press.

Turner, Mary Donovan. 2004. Daughter Zion: Giving Birth to Redemption. Pages 193–204 in *Pregnant Passions*. Edited by Cheryl Kirk-Duggan. Leiden: Brill.

Van Leeuwen, Raymond C. 2003. Form Criticism, Wisdom, and Psalms 111–112. Pages 65–84 in *The Changing Face of Form Criticism for the Twenty-first Century*. Edited by Ehud Ben Zvi and Martin Sweeney. Grand Rapids: Eerdmans.

Weems, Renita. 1995. *Battered Love: Marriage, Sex, and Violence in the Hebrew Prophets*. Minneapolis: Fortress Press.

Weiser, Arthur. 1962. *The Psalms*. Old Testament Library. Philadelphia: Westminster Press.

West, Gerald. 2006. The Poetry of Job as a Resource for the Articulation of Embodied Lament in the Context of HIV and AIDS in South Africa. Paper presented at the Society of Biblical Literature Annual Meeting.

Yee, Gale A. 1992. Hosea. Pages 195–202 in *The Women's Bible Commentary*. Edited by Carol A. Newsom and Sharon K. Ringe. Louisville: Westminster John Knox Press.

———. 2003. *Poor Banished Children of Eve: Women as Evil in the Hebrew Bible*. Minneapolis: Fortress Press.

# Index of Subjects

# Index of Modern Authors

# Index of Scripture References

## DATE DUE

| 3/12/08 | | | |
|---------|---|---|---|
| | | | |
| | | | |
| | | | |
| | | | |
| | | | |
| | | | |
| | | | |
| | | | |
| | | | |
| | | | |
| | | | |
| | | | |
| | | | |
| | | | |

#47-0108 Peel Off Pressure Sensitive

Printed in the United States
94055LV00003B/145/A

9 781589 832473